How to See
and Read the
Human Aura

Judith Collins is a renowned healer, author and educator, and is recognised as Australia's leading authority on the human aura. She established the Earthkeepers Healing Sanctuary, in New South Wales, where she treats many chronically ill patients and people seeking insight into their personal well-being. She also regularly conducts private healing consultations and aura courses in Australia and internationally.

In 1983, Judith Collins was awarded the prestigious Advance Australia Award for her major contribution to the community. In the 1988 Bicentennial celebrations, she was recognised as one of Australia's unsung heroines and her life's work was documented. She appears regularly on television, and can often be heard on radio. She also writes for a number of leading magazines, including *Conscious Living*.

TO MY LOVING MOTHER

She listened.
She did not understand.
But she heard me all the same.

TO JEROME
MY FRIEND IN SPIRIT

He touched my core,
This ancient man of awe.

How to See and Read the Human Aura

Judith Collins

GEDDES & GROSSET

This edition published 2004 by Geddes & Grosset,
David Dale House, New Lanark, ML11 9DJ, Scotland

First published in Australia in 1996 by Thomas C. Lothian Pty Ltd

ISBN 1 84205 345 0

Printed and bound in Poland

FOREWORD

Judith Collins is gifted with a special ability to perceive and diagnose health problems through interpreting the auric field around a person. She has dedicated this talent in service to the thousands of people who come to her for healing and for training.

Since I have been associated with Judith's work, her tireless commitment to helping her clients has made a deep impression on me. She is extremely generous with her time and talent and at the same time very practical and open-minded in referring her clients to other practitioners who may be of assistance.

Judith truly reflects the spirit of Co-Creation in her participation at all the alternative health festivals she attends. She is a great supporter of other practitioners and is a terrific networker. Judith is the most popular speaker at the Conscious Living Expo in Perth, Australia. Her aura workshops and healing circles are booked out every year and she has a standing waiting list for her private consultations. Despite her heavy commitments, Judith still takes time over the four days of the Expo to speak with the stream of people who come to see her on her stand and to give them invaluable advice about their health and life issues. Her down-to-earth approach is a real winner with the public who are often hearing about auras for the first time.

Judith has been a regular contributor to *Conscious Living Magazine* through her articles on the meaning of the aura and how to interpret auras for physical, emotional and spiritual guidance. These articles have been very popular and have demystified a metaphysical approach to healing, which in the past has been discounted as being unscientific and esoteric.

I think Judith's real strength lies is her ability to introduce these advanced healing methods to the average person and she has convinced many doctors of the effectiveness of her healing work especially with terminally ill patients. In the seminars and workshops which Judith conducts, she is able to impart her knowledge about colours and auras in a practical and easy-to-follow way. She interacts with participants on a personal level—often giving them important insights about their personal lives.

I am sure that this book will make a valuable contribution to bridging the information gap about such a profoundly important modality. Congratulations Judith on your service to humanity.

Patricia Hamilton
Publisher
Conscious Living Magazine

CONTENTS

PREFACE

I first stepped out into the public arena to draw and read auras at the Mind, Body and Spirit Festival in Sydney in November 1990. Somewhat nervous and unsure of how I would be accepted, I was wonderfully surprised when I was inundated by people wanting to meet and speak with me. Since then, a wealth of knowledge and experience has flowed through my coloured pencils to the thousands of people who have come my way.

My lectures, courses and healing work have taken me to many countries, opening my mind and exposing my auric eyes to new frontiers. I have witnessed much human experience including: the sickening aura of a refugee in Bosnia; the hard, yet peaceful aura of an elderly man in Ireland; the aura of a tortured young Vietnamese boy; the self-empowered aura of a small Russian community; the pleaful aura of an AIDS victim; the joyful aura of a disabled child.

As we journey together through *How to See and Read the Human Aura* I will share with you my vast experience. You will learn to determine the strength and quality of your eyes and to evaluate your intuitive perception. There are numerous exercises in the book which will stimulate and develop your auric skills. But most of all you will learn that auric perception allows you to make informed choices in all areas of your life.

Literally thousands of people throughout the world have brought about this book. Their relentless pressure on me to take pen to paper to answer their queries and to create a step-by-step instructional handbook has come to fruition. However, it would not have been possible without the help and support of the following people: my husband Paul, who produced the illustrations and painstakingly checked the manuscript at all stages—his constant encouragement and creative inspiration were invaluable; Roslyn Gentles and Irene Phipps for their many ideas and suggestions; all the other people who have supported the book with their personal comments.

I invite you to share with me the fascinating and rewarding insights of the human aura.

1

A PERSONAL JOURNEY

Everything possible to be believed is an image of truth.

William Blake

My earliest memory of seeing auras is approximately at the age of three. It was about this time that I came to realise that I could see the slightest glimmer of light in total darkness, when those around me could not. Insects and my pet cat were easy to detect at night as they were encased in their own electromagnetic field of light. Birds, perched high in the trees, shone like beacons in the black of the night. No detail went unnoticed by my awakened eyes.

Little did I know what I was seeing and that my eyes saw far beyond the vision of others. As I approached school age, my understanding of colour was slowly unfolding, giving me a perceptive form of communication which I could not readily explain. During these innocent years, I was unaware that others could not see the intensity and density of light that was always before me. I was often accused of lying, seeking attention, day dreaming or exaggerating, accusations which served only to lower my self-esteem.

By the time I had reached the age of fourteen I could read the finest details of an aura and interpret it as quickly as a person can read a signpost. However, because the vast majority of people don't view the world in this way, my road of self-development has, at times, proved difficult. I am one of the rare people who has never had the opportunity to get to know someone, because I can read their aura and know them instantly. As a result, I had trouble relating to people outside of my family which caused me to cling to my roots until my early teens.

My family has always been loving and attentive. Laughter, cuddles and an overwhelming degree of togetherness insulated the first thirteen years of my life. I am the only sister to three brothers, who never seemed to be affected by my peculiar way of looking at the world. Instead they helped me to laugh at myself when the going got too rough. My brother, Chris, would sing, 'They're coming to take you away, ha, ha, to the funny farm'. His jovial manner always calmed my fears.

Ours was a creative household. My father building, painting and decorating to the melodic operatic sways of Mario Lanza, while my mother sat at her sewing machine creating an elegant garment, and supervising my father's work. Spontaneously, he would break into poetic verse or nonsensical riddles. As an ex-lifesaver, Dad loved to swim, and in this I was his sole companion. When the family moved out of the suburbs of Sydney to the edge of the countryside, my father introduced me to the delights of swimming in rivers. I can remember how I loved to swim on my back so that I could look at the auras of the surrounding countryside. It was a magic scene and I no longer felt separate and isolated. I was an integral cog, simply partaking of the richness of its wonders.

My eldest brother, Chris, and I have always been good friends. The seven year gap in our ages has made little difference. Undoubtedly we are soulmates brought together to help one another blossom and grow. Our great love of music and theatre led us to copy dance routines from movies of the 1920s through to the 1950s during our teenage years. The Charleston, hootenanny and rock and roll were among our favourites, and we went to dances, theatres and concerts together. In adult years, Chris became the sound engineer for all of my meditation, lecture and self-education cassette recordings, as well as the special effects co-ordinator for the spiritual children's stories I recorded in 1993. He remains the family comedian.

Michael, my second eldest brother, has always been a keen gardener and homemaker and a great help to Mum. During the summer, our dinner table was regularly adorned with the vibrant colours and tantalising aromas of freshly picked salad vegetables, which he had personally grown. I remember his neat, string-lined garden, so lovingly attended that a weed would not dare show itself. It was at this time that I began to notice the compatibility of plants through their auras. Plants whose auric energy patterns appeared twisted and knotted did not grow to full health. However, those that appeared entwined with each other flourished. Such observations sparked my interest in nature, and I soon realised that some plants are just as incompatible as people can be.

My younger brother, Mark, was rather intuitive as a child and was a great comfort to me when we were growing up.

My mother, a talented, creative home decorator, was quick to offer accurate details of the colours that captured my attention. I remember quizzing her over several shades which, at the time, were hard to define. Once when asking her if a colour was either red or brown, I learnt to identify it as terracotta. On trying to distinguish between what appeared to me as a range of browns, my mother carefully defined them as mushroom, fawn, doe-skin and walnut. In our house there was no such thing as brown, blue, green and red. Every variation was recognised in its own right and its appropriate companion explained for either decor, personal attire or landscaping.

When my nursery school teacher instructed the class to draw a tree and colour it green, I was confused. Staring at a blank piece of paper I envisaged an impression of a tree. Its trunk a rich mixture of browns, reds, greys, blues, yellows and orange. Its foliage a combination of greys, greens, yellows, orange, blues, purples and off-whites. So, I put up my hand and enquired as to what shade. The teacher patiently explained that the classroom had a limited number of colour pencils to share, and we just had to make do. When the drawings were complete each child was asked to say a few words about their tree. My turn came and for a moment I was stunned. Then, I stood up and said, 'My tree is not real. It's a pretend tree, because it doesn't have any real tree colours.' Lost for words, the teacher quickly moved on to question another child. I had to face the situation of being misunderstood time and time again during my early school years.

It was no wonder that on my seventh birthday my parents gave me the complete set of Derwent colour pencils, seventy-two in all.

When I was at primary school I learnt the hard way not to speak out about my observations of people's auras. One time, I looked up at the girl sitting in front of me and I felt the colours of her aura suggested that she was either sick or about to wet her pants. I quickly caught the teacher's attention and told her. She questioned the child, but my insight was denied. However, within the next ten minutes there was a puddle on the floor. Unfortunately, I could not contain my laughter and was justly reprimanded by the stern look on the teacher's face. She stared at me bewildered, not understanding me at all.

Several weeks later a boy's wooden pencil case, a birthday present from his father, disappeared. The classroom was searched high and low. A suggestion of theft was put forward by the teacher. I looked about the heads of my classmates to determine the guilty party. I raised my hand and explained to the teacher, 'Peter must have taken it'. I was asked to supply some evidence, and completely stumped, I cried out in my defence, 'I just know.' Peter began to protest, repeatedly denying any connection to the disappearance. He screamed out and called me a liar, and I broke into tears. To restore peace, and to support Peter's innocence, the teacher searched his desk, lunch box and school bag. Nothing was revealed. When she folded his cardigan, which was previously draped over his school bag, the pencil case slid out of one of the sleeves and the class was shocked. Once again the teacher peered at me with wonderment. When she asked me how I knew that Peter had taken the pencil case, I didn't have an answer. When all was said and done, I was made to feel guilty for telling on a classmate, and because I couldn't explain how I knew that Peter was the culprit. By some, my behaviour was seen as revengeful. I began to withdraw into my own world to avoid being questioned and judged—a pattern of behaviour which would reach its climax during my adolescence when I thought that I would never be able to reveal my true self.

I was unsure of myself and turned to the comfort of my doting maternal grandmother who was only too ready to accept me. Whenever I spontaneously read any of her neighbour's auras she would gently pull my nose and say, 'Who's a bright little button?' I suspect that she was aware of my special gift but she died when I was seven so I could never ask her. A conclusion I drew from family reports of my grandfather's inability to wear a watch or carry one on his person, because all clockwork stopped dead in his presence. A phenomenon I now recognise as a forceful electromagnetic aura. I have inherited this trait but with computers not clocks.

A change of primary schools brought with it an air of excitement as well as apprehension. I was becoming skilled in avoiding controversy, and by reading my teacher's aura, I could better fit into the system. I settled in quite well, and even befriended the old catholic nun who taught me, much to the disgust of my classmates. All the kids hated her crabby manner. As quick as a whip, you would feel the stinging thrust of her wooden rule as it made contact with your knuckles. Fortunately for the students, she whirled it through the air more than she touched our flesh. After all, we were only six years old. She instilled the fear of God in us through fearing her personally. No one had a kind word for her. Apparently, in years past the same teacher had taught my Uncle Paul, whose memories confirmed that there had been no change in her character or teaching style.

Such comments heralded the first of my salvation duties. Each day in class I studied her aura. It told me that she had at one time wondered if she had the appropriate ingredients to instil Christ's teachings through her teaching vocation and more recently, her body reeked of physical discomfort. Hence, her personal attitude and focus was, to onlookers, undesirable. In my childish way, I knew and understood her grief, and thus came to love her dearly, but unfortunately she didn't reciprocate my kind intentions.

During the next school year, my understanding of the colourful vibrations and the rays of light I saw around people continued to increase. In particular, Sunday church became the major place for my auric learning. People of all ages and with varying life experiences gathered for devotion. I came to know many of my models intimately while they were totally unaware of my presence. Each week I looked forward to seeing their array of auric colours and patterns, so I could plot their progress.

Sacramental processions, in particular, took my fancy. I recall one occasion when a grand procession of seven- and eight-year-old girls dressed in white, adorned with a white veil and accompanied by boys in complementary attire, moved slowly into the church to make their first holy communion. Their auras were charged with a mixture of nervous tension and spiritual exhaltation. Pinks, purples, pale blue and golden shades combined in the auric pattern of the group.

The vibrant colours of the aura fascinated me. One day as I was waiting for the traffic to clear so that I could cross the road with a girlfriend, I noticed a man from her neighbourhood standing on the opposite side of the road. His aura was dull in light intensity with a dense scattering of black and pale grey flecks and I couldn't work out what this could mean. Some weeks later he died. This was my introduction to learning to read the language of the human aura. Suddenly it took on a new meaning and the colourful, interwoven layers of the aura no longer appeared to me as a childish curiosity or entertainment. I quickly learnt that they portrayed the whole person. Life for me took on a new awareness. Relationships in particular, became more interesting.

Throughout my colour-filled childhood people and rooms played an important role in my personal development. My perception of the human aura grew more accurate as each day passed. Then, at the age of fourteen, I realised that I could read an aura instantly and thoroughly. My life took on a whole new meaning. I became confused and distrustful of everyone around me. I could clearly see and read their strong and weak points, as well as any ulterior motives. I rebelled against life, motivated by a need to set right what was wrong with it.

The Vietnam War was raging at the time. What better cause could I have. Politicians on television's nightly news would sound their opinions while I analysed their aura for the truth. It was during this period I came to realise that I could read auras from television and photographs. I was developing my ability at a rapid pace, but instead of being overjoyed with this gift, I became frustrated, confused and angry. I was so different from other people and felt so alone. My best intentions were always being misunderstood and were definitely not appreciated. It seemed that I was forever telling people what to do, not because I liked to boss them about, but because I could read their aura and understood what was good for them.

My life began to take a turn for the worse, and my family life became a challenge. I loved my family dearly and didn't want to be aware of their innermost secrets. So, I kept my distance, preferring to keep company with casual friends. Looking back at this stage of my life, I realise that rejection was my way of dealing with closeness. Fortunately, my mother never gave up and won me back into her loving arms.

My lifelong ability of seeing and interpreting auras has been checkered with trial and error. Only in my late teens did I really begin to get it right, because true love walked into my heart and I was finally able to begin to be my true self. A few weeks before my eighteenth birthday I met Paul Collins, my husband-to-be. I saw in his aura as we sat opposite each other at a youth council meeting, that we were to be wed. Fortunately, it only took him ten days to reach the same conclusion! So began a chapter of pure bliss—for more than twenty years he has nurtured and encouraged me. His graceful soul is indeed my mentor.

My life has been a fascinating journey to date. Nowadays, I combine my ability to read auras with my spiritual healing skills, to locate and rectify chronic health disorders. The fulfilment that this brings me can be measured by the positive results people find when consulting me. I recall a man in his early fifties who suffered greatly with a rash on his scalp which produced weeping sores. His search for the cause, as well as a cure, had taken him from specialist to specialist, but without success. A quick glance at his aura showed me that the problem stemmed from his kidneys and nervous system, so I set about healing him. What was a simple, straightforward diagnosis to me, proved to be a rewarding experience for him.

I discovered that I had spiritual healing abilities in my mid-thirties. When I place my hands on a person, I simply relax and allow a divine source of healing to work through me to bring my client relief from their suffering. As a service to the public, I established Earthkeepers Healing Sanctuary where I treat the sick and the aimless. Planes have become my second home as I dart back and forth across the states of Australia seeing as many people as I am able to. When I close my eyes to sleep each night, I see all the smiling faces of those who have found a new life through my ability to see auras. This is reward enough for being alive as I think to myself, there by the grace of God, go I.

My world of auras is no longer a lonely one. At last I am free to be my true self and better still, I am loved for it.

2

THE HUMAN AURA

He whose face gives no light shall never become a star.
William Blake

The human aura is not a new age phenomenon or something that originated from a weird cult. It is a living energy that consists of close-knit electromagnetic particles of varying densities, suspended around the body in several layers known as auric bodies. Some of these layers follow the body's contours while others form the shape of an oval, which is commonly known as the auric egg. The aura can be defined in three ways:

- **Absorbent energy** because it is open to exchange with all forms of energy. For example, a walk along a deserted beach in the stillness of the early hours of the morning will soothe and restore your aura as it absorbs the balance and renewal of nature. However, an angry encounter will have the opposite effect, depleting your energy and leaving you shattered and withdrawn.
- **Data energy** because it contains your past, present and future thoughts, feelings and actions, allowing those with the gift of clairvoyancy to read you like a book.
- **Life-force energy** because it exists only while you are alive. During illness it shrinks and fades, in accordance

with the level of disease, and completely disappears when you die. It can also be likened to a mirror by which the person is reflected at every stage of their development.

Since time began, individuals with acute spiritual awareness have recognised and worked with the human aura to heal the sick, domesticate animals, determine weather patterns, communicate with the dead, predict the future and to receive divine inspiration and visions.

The combination of hereditary factors, attitude, life experience and environment creates a vibrating frequency of the close-knit electromagnetic particles, which in turn creates a unique aura for each individual. Because of its oscillating movement, people can either be magnetically drawn towards, or repelled from, each other.

Many forms of man-made energy surround us in this modern, technological world, for example, electricity, microwaves and radio waves. These forms of energy are very different to auric bodies (energies) and have a detrimental effect on the human aura, even in small doses. Natural forms of energy such as wind, light and sound recharge the aura. However, over exposure to any natural energy can result in auric drainage because the individual aura is weak in comparison to the strength of natural energy forces.

An aura presents to the observer an elaborate array of coloured energy lines indicating the process of thought and feeling from moment to moment, and also specific potentialities of the person. It is constantly moving, altering and reshaping itself in response to personal impulses. Colours that represent heightened emotions change rapidly whereas colours representing focus and destiny linger in the aura for months. The radiance of an infant's aura is subtle, indicating newness and self-exploration. In young children, auric colours and patterns become more solid ,indicating instinctive survival, bonding and grounding.

At no other time in life is the aura more scattered, yet evolving, than during adolescence. Colours and patterns represent the change of self-focus as the young person witnesses the development of their physical body, awakening them to their true self. A yearning to be understood, be free of judgement and persecution, a strong will and strong desires, is the auric perception striving to recognise and test out its uniqueness. Developing one's intuitiveness is as attractive as is creative expression through dance, music, art, code of conduct, dress and culture. Life's impressions surface to confront and question one's individuality and to determine a sense of

YOUR AURA REVEALS

GOOD AND POOR HEALTH

VITALITY AND DISEASE

STRONG AND WEAK EMOTIONS

THE ABILITY TO LOVE AND BE LOVED

PERSONAL RELATIONSHIP INVOLVEMENT

FEARS AND STRENGTHS

CREATIVE AND ADDICTIVE PATTERNS

TALENTS AND SKILLS

LEARNING AND ACHIEVEMENT

PERSONAL EVOLVEMENT

GOOD AND POOR EXPERIENCE

SPIRITUAL AWARENESS

SPIRIT GUIDE ATTACHMENT

PAST LIFE EXPERIENCE

and
ALL THAT IS YOU

communal belonging. Such behaviour and self-expression continues until auric development has reached maturity. For the average person this process is over the first twenty-seven years of their life.

When an aura is prevented from maturing through life experience, it remains immature, and this affects all aspects of the personality. A dysfunctional person locked into self-destructive patterns may never realise matured auric balance, and thus never know long-term happiness or settlement.

From the final phase of adolescence to middle age, changes in the aura are caused by the individual's response to life. As we move into advanced years, instinctive perception allows the ageing person to attune to his or her environment like the unborn child. As physical faculties decline, auric perception dramatically increases. The solid auric colour and patterns of day-to-day survival make way for the subtle colours of new life and exploration as we approach the next phase, known as death. At this point the aura has gone its full cycle.

The aura has seven different layers (described below), each with a distinctive role to play in your day-to-day life. Through understanding the role and flow of each part of your aura, you can measure the state of your whole being, as well as how people and circumstances around you are positioned for your personal growth and learning, and your inner knowing will be awakened.

The seven auric bodies

The physical auric body

The physical layer is closest to the body and represents good and poor health. When you instinctively feel a friend is not in the best of health, your perception is detecting this layer of the aura. It is usually seen by observers as a bright white, milky yellow or very pale blue band beginning at the edge of the skin

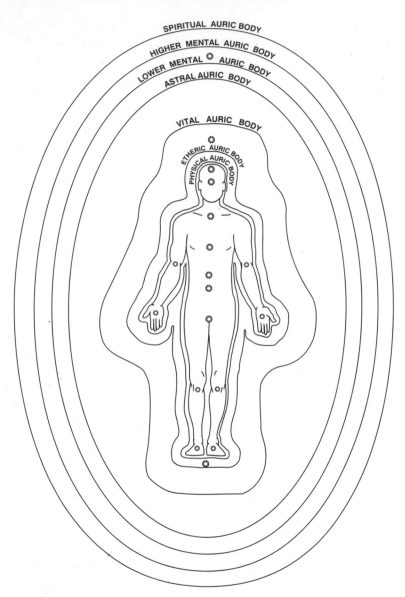

THE LAYERS OF THE HUMAN AURA

and extending outwards for approximately three centimetres. The fact that the energy particles of the aura are unique in each individual provides the means by which animals can track a group of human beings or a specific individual. The acute senses of an animal connect with both the electromagnetic particles of physical layer of the aura as well as the scent of the body. Cats, dogs and horses, in particular, have been known to raise the alarm that their owners are sick or trapped in pain.

Good health is depicted by a uniform bright band of light surrounding and contouring the entire body. When a person is brimming with health the physical auric frequency can easily be seen around the head and hands.

Poor health is indicated by a bulge in the physical layer near the affected area. It looks a bit like the lumps and bumps in a bowl of poorly mixed porridge. Old injuries sustained in childhood can often be detected at this level. My husband, a natural health practitioner, became frustrated at not being able to relieve a client's pain, so he called on me. I looked at the client and explained how he had hurt his head during a water sporting accident over ten years ago. Shocked and dumbfounded, the client slowly uttered his confirmation. Apparently he had been severely dunked when water skiing and hit on the head with a ski. His current pain was not responding to treatment because of underlying layers of internal bruising. With specific additional information my husband was able to treat his client's neck and shoulder appropriately.

In chronic illnesses, such as cancer and chronic fatigue, the bulge in the physical layer may extend into the etheric and vital layers, as such illnesses also involve emotional responses, which are depicted in these layers.

Hereditary disorders can also be located in the physical layer. While sitting in a pub in Dublin with my Irish publisher friend Declan White, and world famous metaphysical teacher, Stuart Wild, a man named Brian came up to us. Stuart immediately asked, 'How come you're still so slim after all these years,' and pointed to his own tummy bulge. Brian shrugged his shoulders. I laughed and said, 'Oh Stuart, if you could see auras, you would know that Brian has a hereditary digestive and stomach disorder. I bet the whole family is lean.' Brian, mesmerised by my correct findings, sidled up to me for additional information and the remedy.

The physical auric body can be recorded through the process of Kirlian photography, invented by the Russian scientists Valentina and Semyon Kirlian. A person places each hand on a plate-electrode, which is then stimulated by a high-frequency spark generator for a few moments, to produce the auric image of the hand on film. The strength of the image portrayed will depend on your health and well-being. In a strong aura, such as my own, long, dense, black sprays of energy can be seen emanating from my finger tips, indicating my healing ability as well as good health.

The etheric auric body

The etheric layer, unlike any other layer of the aura, is two-tiered. The first tier is a replica of the physical body and an integral part of the total aura. It is seen as a silvery, blue-grey mist contouring the body, and extends ten centimetres from the physical auric layer. The second tier appears as a mass of luminous colours. It is overshadowed by the first tier, and depicts the eternal self, thus it accompanies an individual from one life to another. Its role is to memorise (via the subconscious mind) a person's entire life and to carry off the soul at the point of death. Under hypnotic trance, the mind can be coaxed to glean information from the second tier of the etheric aura, thus revealing experiences of childhood and past lifetimes. Whenever the conscious or unconscious mind engages in discussion, images from the past may appear in the aura. While I was speaking to a young woman who longed to visit the Scandinavian countries, her etheric aura produced an image of her past life self—a peasant woman of viking origin.

Some gifted clairvoyants are able to perceptively penetrate this layer and clearly read its memory bank.

As your auric vision becomes more accurate, it will see through the silvery blue-grey haze of the first tier, and observe the luminous splashes of the vibrant colours of the second tier. The following examples relate to the nature of the etheric layer.

The phantom limb syndrome

The phantom limb syndrome is associated with the etheric layer of the aura. Because this layer is an exact replica of your body and remains whole at all times, people who have lost a limb often experience a clear sense of the limb remaining intact long after it has been removed. As the physical auric layer indicates this loss to the etheric aura, over a period of time, the sensation passes. Therefore, the etheric aura is an indicator of what is happening at the very fundamental level of a person's being.

Near death experience

Near death experience accounts explain the sensations of the second tier of the etheric aura when it separates from the body and hovers beyond the material reality. The person seems suspended in time and may look at their body, for example, lying on an operating table, and wonder how they can be in two places at the same time, never realising that they have an etheric double, equipped with memory. Over the years I have helped many people understand what they experienced while drifting between life and death.

When your body dies, the soul is transported by the etheric aura into a non-physical world where it has the opportunity to reacquaint itself with family and friends, and to connect to an emanation of love, which we know as God. People declared clinically dead who are then resuscitated, frequently recount such an experience as they describe their out-of-body adventure.

Bilocation

Bilocation is the projection of the etheric double of a living human being to a place or person at another location. In some ancient religions, disciples spent years mastering the technique. Today, many seek to develop this ability through meditation and specially designed exercises. However, enlightened people don't require training. The skill is inherent with their expanding connectiveness to the realms of Heaven and Earth.

In the last century, an Italian Franciscan priest, Padre Pio, lived in a monastery at San Giovanni Rotondo, but appeared to people in different parts of the world in order to heal them. Sai Baba, a divinely charismatic Indian teacher and healer, regularly supports his disciples throughout the world via bilocation. He has been known to appear to a large number of his followers as they gathered for meditation or discussion.

Spirits, ghosts and divine apparitions

Spirits, ghosts and divine apparitions have been experienced through the ages by those with acute intuitive awareness. Their heightened perception penetrates the reality of the material world, allowing them to see and communicate with the etheric replicas of deceased beings.

A client of mine recounted to me such an experience. While in the kitchen making a cup of coffee she felt that someone was watching her. She turned around and saw her daughter standing very still with a dazed smile on her face. She was whispering repeatedly, 'Goodbye Mum, I'll always love you.' As my client began to question her, her daughter's image faded. During the moments that followed she felt that her imagination had run wild. Twenty minutes later there was a knock on the front door. It was the police. They reported a fatal car accident in which her daughter was killed instantly. She realised then that her daughter had come home to say goodbye before passing over to the other side.

While this is not an uncommon story, there are many

people who don't wish to accept the reality that the spirit realm live among us, lending us guidance and support every day. Everyone has a guardian spirit, who is only too willing to facilitate intimate communication and unconditional friendship.

Several years ago, St Jerome appeared at the foot of my bed and spoke to me in the early hours of a spring morning. Dressed in a ragged, frayed tunic, his bony, half-starved figure, with its long, thin grey beard, was an etheric double of his former self. The words he uttered were precise and articulate. He had come to offer me inspiration and support until the year 2003, whereupon our work together would be complete.

The vital auric body

The vital layer displays radiant splashes of coloured light of varying frequencies within the contour of the body and can extend up to thirty centimetres from the etheric layer. The vital auric body, one's true life-force, is the only layer of the aura that is a two-way energy system. It radiates energy and absorbs it from the surrounding environment, whereas the other layers of the aura only absorb energy.

When in true communion with nature, you can feel its tranquil life-force touch your soul. It is then that you know that your vital auric body is absorbing nature's energy to revitalise itself. As the experience is aurically interpreted by the senses, you may feel relaxed or invigorated, renewed or recharged. But whatever you feel, nature's balance will deliver an inner contentment to the deepest part of your being, and you will make peace with yourself. Your responses to life are shaped through the vital layer. Personality, emotions, self-image and personal vitality are depicted at this level of the aura.

The vital aura expands when a person is excited and shrinks when a person is sad or depressed, thus emotions are felt at this level. When you feel that the world is closing in on you, it is the vital auric body exhibiting a degree of weakness.

If a person directs their anger at you and it is not processed thoroughly at the astral auric level, it will be absorbed by the vital aura and disrupt its interactive behaviour. Furthermore, when the energies of the vital layer do not flow, body tissues begin to decay. However, this kind of permanent damage to the aura takes many years of self-abuse.

In the moments, days or even some weeks before death approaches, the vital aura is devoid of colour, a sure indication that the individual is not long for this life. Conversely, individuals who have achieved self-fulfilment in their life goals, career or spiritual enlightenment, shine like beacons in a fog. When in their presence there is a certain charisma that seems to charge the atmosphere.

In November 1993, while I was working at the Conscious Living Expo in Western Australia, I was drawing a man's aura, when I suddenly felt a surge of energy tugging on the back of my head, as though someone were reaching out to me. Automatically, I extended my left hand towards my back and instantly felt the warmth and weight of a man's hand. Within seconds my sixth sense recognised an enlightened being. Fixed in a trance, I turned to face him. We didn't speak but stared into each other's eyes while our auras interchanged, speaking a language that only they understood. Someone spoke and the magic moment came to a sudden end.

His aura was vibrant, exhibiting an abundance of self-esteem and the strength of a phoenix rising from the ashes. As he walked away from me, one of the show organisers asked me if I knew who he was and I shook my head in ignorance. The mystery man was Robert Kiyosaki, lecturer, author and self-made millionaire, born in Hawaii, now residing in Arizona. In 1979, he faced financial ruin. By 1990, at age forty-three, he was financially secure so that he would never have to work again. Since 1982, as a founding director of the Accelerated Learning Institute, he has been teaching many of the principles of creating wealth throughout the world. His students include some of the world's leading educators, trainers and leaders.

The following day, while I was deeply engaged in drawing an elderly man's aura, I suddenly lifted my head from the paper and shouted, 'Robert?' 'No, I'm Kim, his wife,' came the excited reply. I had recognised her husband's aura within her own. When we share our lives with other people, at home or at work, a part of the company we keep is absorbed by the vital auric body. Hence, when you visit a clairvoyant you can expect to hear something about how those with whom you share your life are affecting your life-force.

The astral auric body

The astral layer is the first place where good and bad life experiences have an effect. It forms a coloured oval shape around the body, and is known as the auric egg. It extends approximately ten to sixty centimetres from the outer edge of the vital layer. It is not easily viewed by the novice observer, but is readily accessible to psychic perception. Some people who can see auras with ease have never seen this layer.

I always refer to the astral auric body as a 'blender', mixing and churning individual ingredients to create a whole substance. To me, this is the easiest way to understand its role. Whenever three or more people are in close proximity their astral auras go into action, blending and kneading, to produce a smooth balance for mutual interaction. Aurically, we all give and take what we need without question or conscious recognition, from whatever energy source is in close contact. At this level of the aura, all forms of energy affect you: people, plants, light, sound, electricity and so on, and the astral layer absorbs as much as it can. This is why the health and wellbeing of people and animals who reside near power generation stations or dense overhead power lines is affected over a period of time. In these situations, I can imagine how the astral aura, whose job it is to ensure electromagnetic harmony, becomes confused and frustrated by foreign electrical currents.

HOW THE ASTRAL AURA WORKS

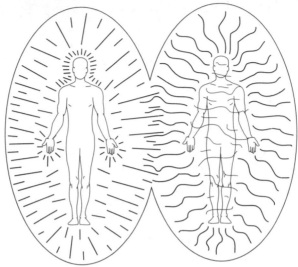

A charismatic aura (left) blends with an emotionally confused aura (right).

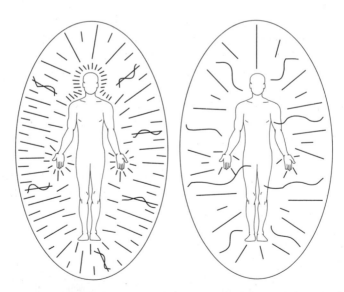

The charismatic aura (left) has absorbed and processed the emotionally confused aura's energy and projected healing energy, enabling the emotionally confused aura to stabilise.

The aura is very sociable at the astral level, freely exchanging its energy with others. Firstly, it combines with those who share its home life, to form what is known as a family aura. This then expands and connects with the auras of neighbours, creating a neighbourhood aura, which in turn connects to the community aura and forms a social aura. This connects with atmospheric forces and transmutes to a global aura.

Every day of your life you come across examples that show how the astral aura works. At the start of a bus or train trip you may be brimming with contentment. However, by the time you arrive at your destination, your mood and energy levels have altered, leaving you feeling washed out. While on your journey you were in the company of people who are emotionally suppressed or depressed and their negative energy has drained away your positive energy. Should you repeatedly find yourself in this situation, practise the aura strengthening exercises, so that you keep your aura in balance. The opposite situation can also occur, where you start the trip feeling restless and depressed while everyone else is brimming with contentment. As this transfers to you, you are uplifted.

Cults and social beliefs are locked into social astral auras. Next time you are walking down a city street take a look at the style of hair and attire of adolescents. During these impressionable, developmental years the astral aura succumbs to various persuasions.

Riots are another example of the united communal power of astral auras. One angry person may catch the attention of several slightly disgruntled people, igniting their discontent. Together they explode into a violent frenzy. Before long more and more embittered people join them. Suddenly a non-violent person can perform the most violent acts, swayed along by the astral communal auric waves.

Interestingly, polling days are affected by social astral auras. Those known as 'swinging voters' and 'fence-sitters' are likely to be swept up by the most dominant social aura at the polling booth and vote according to its persuasion.

Astral auric blending doesn't have to be a negative experience. Relaxing in a meditation or healing circle for three minutes or more, facilitates the transfer of energy for collective harmonious focus. This peaceful and unplifting auric interaction heightens intuitive expression and empowers spiritual growth. I advise families who are experiencing loss or disruption to sit together peacefully in a circle for twenty minutes, with their eyes closed, focusing on a positive resolution.

Past and present day life information is contained in the astral aura. Déjà vu is a constant reminder that the astral aura is aware of your total life experience. The moment it identifies a person or a place, a message of recognition is sent to the mind. The intrigue begins when you consciously try to assess the memory. When consulting a hypnotherapist, so-called lost or buried memories of childhood may be coaxed from the astral aura as the mind relaxes and signals that it is safe to do so.

A young man named Michael had been adopted at birth. While he held no resentment towards his biological mother, disappointment, coupled with a sense of abandonment, was always with him. He had an innate fear of emotionally hurting people and therefore allowed himself to be hurt instead.

I sat with Michael as my hypnotherapist friend and colleague, Klaus Reiher, took his consciousness back to the womb. There, Michael was able to feel his mother and assess the situation in which she found herself. Awakening from the trance, he wept solidly as he described how much she had wanted to keep him. This was all he needed to know in order to get on with his life. Some weeks later he ended an emotionally debilitating relationship with a long-term girlfriend, who had been suffocating his creative talent.

When a clairvoyant describes relatives and friends or tells of emotional traumas you've encountered, the information is being gleaned from the astral auric layer because of its interaction with family and friends. A woman, who had sought healing for her hip, proceeded to describe her ailment to me. Cutting her short, I enquired about her son's nasal problem. I was able to accurately pinpoint the ailment because they shared the same dwelling and as a direct consequence their astral auras had interchanged.

Prospective suicide first displays itself in the astral auric layer. The naturally vibrant colours of the astral layer become dull. As the person becomes more and more depressed the astral aura presses on the vital aura, curbing its flow and preventing all means of salvation.

The magnetic oscillation of the astral aura allows us to become infatuated with each other, inviting people to fall in and out of love. True love, the type that lasts for eternity, occurs when the astral auric body moulds two auras into one.

When you are in tune with your astral auric body, it can deliver the richness of all that is good in the world and enrich your life.

The lower mental auric body

The lower mental layer displays a person's abilities on the conscious or intellectual level. It extends five to twenty centimetres from the astral aura and is yellow in colour. Varying shades of yellow depict the degree of well-being and focus of an individual. A rich golden yellow energy can be seen pulsating when the mind is stimulated.

One evening when I was working at the Mind, Body and Spirit Festival in Sydney some years ago, people kept passing by my stall with beaming yellow energy rays around their heads. My curiosity was aroused. Finally, I realised that the neighbouring office blocks had ceased trading and that their staff were overflowing into the festival. Computer operators, accountants, solicitors, bankers, secretaries and clerks were out in force. Obviously they had not completely shut down from the day's work.

I have used this layer of the aura to help my clients to understand possible career choices and to develop self-counselling and appropriate affirmation techniques. But beware, the lower mental aura is, at times, so closely intertwined with the astral aura that it's difficult for the novice observer to separate the two. When this circumstance arises, it takes skill and patience to interpret these levels of the aura accurately.

Frequently I encounter clients who dream of achieving great goals, but despite their every effort, face constant failure. Eventually they reach the conclusion that something of which they are unaware is blocking them. After a few moments of discussion and observation of the lower mental aura, I am able to highlight the beliefs or fears inhibiting their progress. People are then better equipped to help themselves.

The lower mental aura also reveals when a person is fooling him or herself. At festivals and the courses which I conduct, people often tell me of their own clairvoyant abilities. One glance at their aura and I can determine whether or not they are genuine. Young children are often brought to me by their parents because of their tales of communication with a deceased relative or imaginary friend. I've had some very interesting conversations with children.

A twelve-year-old girl reported to her parents that she could not sleep because in the early hours of the night she could hear the murmur of voices and occasionally she would be shown a table and a drinking glass turned upside down. When I heard this, I realised that someone in the spirit realm was trying to communicate with her family. I studied her lower mental aura to determine whether or not wishful imagination was governing the experience. I was convinced that she was telling the truth when I saw spirit activity in her higher mental aura. Consequently, I sent the family to a spiritualist church where they could be educated in the ways of communicating with the spirit world. The young girl has the gift of mediumship which needs to be carefully nurtured, as I know only too well the trauma that occurs for the untrained and unsupervised.

It is interesting that children in the first ten years of their life use the lower mental aura to manipulate encounters that cross their paths. At birth, infants will often use tears and screams to gain attention, in order to have their needs met. During this period, parents worry about their child's health and contentment until they master a method of communication. Playing one parent against the other is a well-known ploy. As children grow they learn what is and what isn't acceptable behaviour, and also what does and what doesn't bring an appropriate response.

Once I was placed in a very awkward situation while in my local supermarket. A one-year-old boy was sitting in the shopping trolley sobbing desperately. His young, inexperienced mother shouted at him to shut up. I could see that her frustration arose from an inability to see what he was complaining about. Following a moment of hesitation, I told her of his earache and guided her hand to feel the heat in that area. She looked puzzled as she held her son close, embarrassed as she thanked me. Usually when in public I don't intervene in other people's problems, but in this case the child's suffering was pulling on my heart strings.

As we grow from childhood to adolescence and then into adulthood, the astral and lower mental auras level out to provide harmony between the emotions and the intellect. Most people, on reaching their thirtieth year, have achieved quite a degree of balance in their lives. As we progress into old age this balance becomes more noticeable. However, more commonly I am witnessing how the stress of modern civilisation is causing the pendulum to swing back and forth. Career-minded people often cling to their intellect and deny emotional sustenance. Other frustrated individuals cling to twisted emotions, blocking the balance of intellect. Sparks of amber rays appear in the lower mental aura when a person's thinking is focused on overwhelming life issues. Red rays, initiated by the emotions at the astral auric level, indicate deep-seated anger. When they penetrate the lower mental layer they frustrate the ability to think clearly. Grey rays, also arising from the astral aura, indicate that the person is locked into self-pity. The darker the rays the closer the person is to suicide.

A few years ago I was summoned by a woman to visit a nearby hospital to determine why her husband had not come out of a coma following an accident. I searched his aura for reasons and located in the lower mental level a fear of crippling injury. In short, he was too frightened to wake up for fear of being seriously incapacitated. I informed his wife of the problem and suggested ways in which she and the family could help. I conducted some healing to dissolve a blood clot on the man's brain which I found during my observations. The family kept a vigil near his bedside, repeatedly assuring him of his well-being, so that the lower mental aura would activate other auric layers to speed up his recovery. Within twelve hours he was conscious.

Mental illness causes a lack of symmetry to the oval shape of the lower mental aura. It looks as if it has been stretched out of shape and, at times, frayed at the edges. Severe mental illness is depicted by auric polyps which grow between the astral and lower mental auras.

The higher mental auric body

It has taken years of experience for my eyes to penetrate and see the higher mental layer. Its intense energy vibrates at a high frequency which is difficult for the eyes to capture. It expands up to sixty centimetres from the lower mental aura.

When you meditate and reach a level of divine inspiration, you have accessed the higher mental aura. Its purpose is to facilitate the transfer of formless information to the lower mental aura for interpretation by way of thought, feeling, colour, sound, aroma or symbol. The higher mental aura has direct access to Universal Wisdom which anyone can draw upon to enhance talents and to balance the mind, body and spirit. This is why inventors on either side of the world may unknowingly work on the same project. Both release their inventions within weeks of each other and are hailed for their ingenuity.

Individuals with an acute sense of awareness of self or life can easily tap into the inspirational source of the higher mental aura. Artists, musicians, singers, writers, inventors, skilled surgeons, educators, and entrepreneurs are among the many who, through their search to make a difference to the world, automatically open an access to universal knowledge which in turn stimulates and inspires them onwards.

Determined individuals in need of healing can also activate and connect to the higher mental auric body, setting about a chain reaction of spontaneous healing down through the various layers of the aura. John, a client of mine in his late fifties, proudly told me his story. He had not felt well for a few weeks and decided to visit his doctor. Extensive tests were carried out to determine the elusive cause. The prognosis was stomach cancer. When his doctor described the proposed gruesome treatments and the limited hope that accompanied them, John decided to heal himself. He read extensively on diet, nutrition and the cause of cancer, as well as about various natural healing modalities. He then visited a news agency and scanned health magazines in search of healers' advertisements. He also enrolled in a meditation course and learnt to harness the power of his mind.

Three months later he was cured. A change in diet and attitude, plus the power of the mind, had healed him. Proud of his achievements, he returned to his doctor and insisted that he be tested again. The results did not reveal any trace of cancer, however, they did show an overall improvement in his health.

Trance channellers, through deep relaxation and the ability

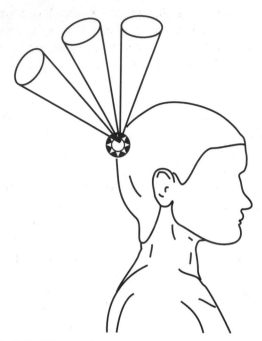

COMMUNICATION WITH THE SPIRIT REALM

The causal chakra is activated by the spirit realm for
communication, which is observed in the higher and lower mental
layers of the aura. When a spirit guide is in communication,
colourful cone-shaped rays emanate from the causal chakra.

to float their conscious mind, are able to open their higher
mental aura so that spirits can communicate with their living
relatives, or deliver advice or enlightenment. When spirit
communication is taking place, the sanctity of the spirit stimulates the higher mental layer of the aura, causing it to radiate
silvery-gold sprays of light to form a glorious halo around the
head of the medium or mystic.

Several years ago I was a keynote speaker at a regional
gathering for members of the spiritualist churches. After my
segment there was a coffee break followed by a trance channelling session by a medium. As always, I watched intently so I

wouldn't miss the magnificent auric colour display that adorns the head of a medium when he or she is moving through the transition of mind and body to spirit. I watched and waited, but nothing happened. The medium began to speak with a foreign accent. Apparently the spirit guide was a wise and ancient Oriental. Startled by what I saw I focused on the lower mental aura to confirm my suspicions. Unfortunately, the medium was attuned to his own imagination that evening. Perhaps in the past he could access his spirit guide, but that evening the spirit was nowhere in sight.

A trance medium myself, I am always fascinated to meet my peers as we are a rare breed, so to speak. A well-known American channeller came to Sydney and allowed her spirit guide to deliver his message to a large Australian audience. At the close of the session, she asked the organisers to direct her to me, as her spirit guide wished us to meet and exchange information.

My introduction to trance channelling came as a surprise. My sister-in-law and I sought to learn how to deepen our meditative consciousness for stress management and relaxation. During the first session, I dropped to such a depth of meditative consciousness that seven spirits took advantage and came through me to address the group. When I returned to consciousness, the group explained what had happened. For several months, I was filled with anxiety and reluctance to release control of myself during meditation, causing great difficulty in relaxation. Then St Jerome appeared to me at the foot of my bed. Thus began the fabulous public working relationship that we both enjoyed for many years.

With his permission I arranged for one of our public appearances to be filmed so that I could analyse the changes in my aura in his presence. The natural violet and dark blue haze of the higher mental aura expanded into the transparent pearly white of the spiritual aura. As I moved into the trance, the colour of the aura was distant from my body. This changed dramatically as I surrendered mental control. The causal chakra, situated at the back of the head, was ablaze with lilac and gold light, and an apricot haze clouded my face. The crown chakra, situated at the top of the head, and the third eye chakra of the brow, had expanded into one spiralling magenta light. A sight to behold!

When spirit guides attach to the aura to give guidance and inspiration, their status and role is easily determined by the colours seen emanating from the causal chakra at the back of the head. Royal blue indicates that the spirit is a deceased relative. Dark green indicates that the spirit has known the person in a past life. Purple, gold or silver represent an angelic being. Coloured sprays radiating from the causal chakra connection detail the supportive nature of the spirit guide. For instance, royal blue with a spray of red shows that the spirit is a deceased relative helping the person to create a new lease on life.

Most people can tap into their higher mental aura at certain times of heightened awareness during their life, but few are able to access it on a day-to-day basis.

The spiritual auric body

The spiritual layer draws on all of the cosmic energy used for earthly life. It enters at the crown chakra and is processed to the numerous chakras (or energy centres) around the body, for distribution to the area which needs assistance. These inner energy centres act like conductors, processing and distributing auric energy to the various layers of the aura. Commonly, the spiritual aura is recognised as the connection to God or Universal consciousness. It is not readily visible to the physical eye, and is seen as a mother-of-pearl white light, encased in a transparent gold shell.

I wasn't able to see the spiritual auric body for many, many years. This soon changed when I advanced in my healing knowledge and work. As my clients experienced spontaneous healings of chronic and terminal illnesses, I witnessed this miraculous force in full operation. Misty sprays of gold light filtered through the various layers of their auras and remained there for up to four days. Then, just as suddenly as it appeared, it disappeared, leaving the person with the sense of rebirth.

Those who attend my aura course come to know this layer as 'the battery pack', a nickname I have given it because of its ability to revitalise people. While I was watching the Barcelona Olympic Games on television, the marathon caught my attention. One of the entrants' spiritual auric body sent a force of energy through his entire aura, revitalising the vital and physical auric bodies, facilitating his win.

When people are in a life-threatening situation and it is not their time to die, a message is sent from the vital auric body to the spiritual auric body, which automatically switches on its life-giving energy. One of my clients fell asleep at the wheel of his car and crashed at great speed into a tree on the side of the road. Although the impact was enough to crush his chest and kill him, he remained conscious. A woman in a blue cape came to the window and told him to close his eyes and go to sleep while she sought help. Believing her to be a passerby, he followed her instructions. As he tried to relax and relieve his pain, a warm tingling sensation moved throughout every part of his body. Within moments he was free of pain and felt very light-headed. Sleep overcame him. When he awoke in hospital, he was surrounded by medical practitioners and his family.

Years later, he sought healing from me, and during the first healing session his spirit guide, a lady dressed in a blue cape, appeared to me. He sat quietly as I recounted her story. Tears flowed down his face as he realised that this was the lady who had saved his life and he could finally thank her. Today he is aware that she truly is his guardian angel.

People who survive being buried alive or being trapped for a period of longer than ten days without water and little oxygen have, without a doubt, experienced the power of the spiritual auric body.

It seems that we rarely use the spiritual auric body at its full force. Our mind, alone, cannot access it. This requires the balance of mind, body and spirit in humility to open its pearly gate, the gateway to all knowing and unconditional love. I suspect that Christ, Buddha, St Francis of Assisi and other divine individuals lived within their spirit bodies, and could therefore commune with the forces of nature, universal wisdom and grace. Daily conscious awareness of the God of creation and the God within comes through the spiritual auric body when the balance of mind and spirit is perfected.

The inner energy (chakras)

The spinning, cone-shaped energy centres known as chakras are an integral part of the auric body. They absorb and distribute its vibrant energy to different parts of your physical body and are partially responsible for its maintenance. You could say that they supply the body with its life-force. When one or more chakras malfunctions or becomes blocked, depression and/or disease usually follows.

There are nine major chakras which are approximately seven to eight centimetres in diameter. Numerous minor chakras, approximately two to three centimetres in diameter, are scattered about the physical body. Each chakra has a specific colour role to play in relation to the body's organs and their well-being. However, the colours of the chakras have no impact on the colours of the aura. I have discussed below the fourteen chakras, nine major and several of the minor, which are easily seen in the human aura. (See the illustration for their positions on page 46.)

Earth chakra (minor)

Dark brown in colour. Seated approximately twenty centimetres beneath the feet. Consequently, as you walk barefoot on the grass the chakra becomes imbedded in the earth, producing a sense of connectiveness. It governs bonding and a sense of community.

Foot chakra (minor)

Brown in colour. Regulates the flow of the body's energies from the physical aura to the outer layer of the spiritual aura. It governs balance, wholeness and the logic mind.

Knee chakra (minor)

Maroon in colour. Centred at the back of each knee, it monitors the flow of the body's energies and governs strength of purpose plus shoulder and neck muscles.

Hand chakra (minor)

Lemon yellow in colour. Centred in the palm of each hand, it governs creative learning and expression.

Root chakra (major)

Red in colour. Seated at the base of the spine. It represents the 'earth' element and gives a sense of being planted firmly on the ground. It governs the adrenals, kidneys, spinal column and solid matter of the body: teeth, nails and bones. The sense of smell is also associated with the root chakra.

Sacral centre (major)

Orange in colour. It is in direct line with the sacrum on the spine and gives a sense of the smooth flow of the self. It relates to the water of the body: urine, vaginal fluids, semen and saliva. I have noticed in my healing work that clients who are blocked at this level have varying degrees of arthritis or

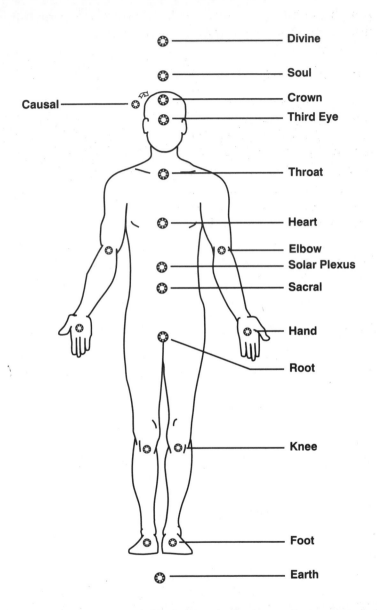

THE CHAKRAS

pain due to friction. The sacral chakra governs the reproductive system, gonads, pelvic area and bladder.

Solar plexus chakra (major)

Yellow in colour. Located on the spine at the level of the stomach. Here we experience warmth, joviality and quality of expansiveness. Its fiery element relates to the brightness of what we see. One moment we can see our life as full and satisfying, but the next moment we see it as mundane and unsuccessful. The solar plexus governs the pancreas, liver, gall bladder, stomach, nervous system, appendix, diaphragm, large intestine and part of the small intestine.

When a client complains to me of sluggishness, the solar plexus is blocking their ability to take up the nourishment of their food intake. Hence, no fire to kindle the flame of life!

Heart chakra (major)

Green in colour. Located on the spine at the level of the breastbone. It represents the air element. At this level you experience airiness, mobility, lightness, gentleness and social interaction. Therefore relationships have a major impact on this chakra. In my work with AIDS sufferers, I have noticed that the heart chakra is usually blocked. It governs the circulatory system, vagus nerve, thymus gland, heart and blood.

Throat chakra (major)

Blue in colour. Positioned on the spine at the level of the throat. Here we experience the sense of solitude. It is a vital link between expression and thought. It represents the ability to communicate with the world around us. It can be gentle and caring. When there is a poor flow of energy in this region you may be over-critical of others and disrespectful of other's opinions. Most throat conditions that I have healed fall into two categories: those who don't speak up for themselves and those who have too much to say. The two extremes seem to affect one's health. The throat chakra governs the thyroid, bronchial and vocal apparatus, lungs and alimentary canal.

Third eye chakra (major)

Indigo in colour. Also known as the Brow Centre due to its position at the point on the forehead, approximately between the eyebrows. This is the level at which the intuitive, imaginative and spontaneous self is linked to the mortal self of mind. It represents the power to materialise thought. For example, you are unhappy at work and feel that you need a change. The next morning you see the perfect job advertised in the newpaper. You are selected for an interview during which you are offered the job.

The third eye governs the pituitary gland, left eye, lower brain, ears, nose, mouth and nervous system. I have noticed that in childless couples, one or both partners have stifled their imaginative self due to restrictions of one sort or another, which causes a block in the third eye. When successfully treated, a child may be conceived.

In the intuitively aware person, this chakra is expanded with rays of indigo penetrating several layers of the aura.

Crown chakra (major)

Violet-pearl in colour. Situated at the top of the head in alignment with the pineal gland. It is the mystical, spiritual link to God. When a person is enlightened, the crown chakra radiates a violet-pearl glow around the head area, commonly recognised as a halo. The size, shape and pattern of the halo is determined by the focus of the higher mental

THE AURIC HALO

Dense light emanations around the head depict the state of health, spirituality and evolvement of a person. This is the easiest part of the aura to see because of the strong focus of the mind. As a person becomes more balanced and spiritually aware, the aura around the head expands. The illustrations below show some of the patterns seen in an auric halo.

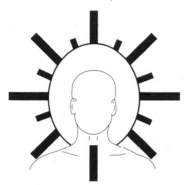

Enlightenment: the outer sprays of light show the expansion of the material consciousness into a higher consciousness.

Devout: the cross configuration of light depicts a Christian commitment to God through prayer.

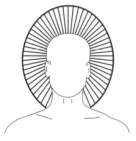

Connected to nature: the inner sprays of light display a communion with nature, where the person feels at one with Creation.

Good health: the waves of light indicate a balance of mind, body and spirit through the alignment of all the auric layers.

auric layer. When a person is in excellent health, the crown chakra irradiates waves of light. A person who is able to communicate with the spirit realm can expand their mind to the level of the crown chakra and to connect with a divine force, whereupon messages flow forth. The crown chakra governs the pineal gland, the right eye and the upper brain.

Causal chakra (minor)

Transparent silver colour. Situated high up, at the back of the head, it facilitates communication between the spirit and the material realms.

Soul chakra (major)

Transparent pearl colour. Situated approximately eight centimetres above the centre of the head. It provides a force of energy via the crown and third eye chakras to inspire you in your day-to-day activities. I believe it recharges the soul, thus keeping a person balanced during stressful encounters.

Divine chakra (major)

Transparent gold colour. Its distance above the soul chakra varies between individuals. Its function is to maintain a permanent link to creation and to the creator. When we die, this chakra expands fully to ensure our return to the spirit realm.

During the process of meditation the chakras open and contract, displaying a beautiful array of colour that looks something like a peacock's tail feathers when fanned. Energy is like water, it follows the least resistance. As the muscles relax and the thinking process quietens, the physical layer of the aura spills over into the etheric layer, giving rise to the sense of self-expansion. The body senses begin to tingle and warm as your consciousness connects to the etheric layer and expands into all other levels of the aura. When the consciousness connects with the higher mental layer, which in turn stimulates the spiritual auric bodies, inspiration, as well as divine guidance, flows freely.

The only time that this process occurs differently is when a person is suffering from a physical or emotional illness, or both. The consciousness, on reaching a state of relaxation, locks into the physical layer of the aura and focuses healing from it to the material body. An individual will usually feel this energy exchange as a sudden, sharp pain that passes rapidly. It also causes tight muscles to twitch as they release their hold on the skeletal body. A warm flow of energy can be felt around the diseased areas of the body.

Meditation not only relaxes the body and frees it from degenerative stress, it also creates a peaceful mind which facilitates the balance of mind and body, as well as evolvement of the soul.

Relationships and the aura

As already discussed, the human aura is a blueprint of how you act, the way you think and feel, as well as your memories, dreams and aspirations. Because every living human being and animal perceives auras instinctively, your aura becomes a walking, talking advertisement of who you have been, who you are now, and who you will be in the future.

The sadness that I see in the average human aura never ceases to astound me. I have come to believe that we live in a society of the 'walking wounded'. Relationships have touched, twisted and devastated so many individuals that there is no doubt in my mind that counselling will become an integral part of survival in a progressive society. Loneliness is ripe, and more and more people are seeking the means of self-healing, and increasing their awareness in search of balance.

When I was growing up, I came to expect to see the inner war of the aura as it coped with the complications most adults impose on themselves as they become entangled in the web of life. But now, to my great disappointment, an increasing number of children, from infants to adolescents, are showing the tell-tale shades of loss and separation in their auras. Pockets of anger born out of frustration and confusion overshadow their creativity, productivity and true self-expression. Some outwardly display this as shyness, withdrawal or nervousness, others as aggression, abrasiveness or uncooperativeness. Either way, the sadness seeps into all aspects of the aura.

When I walk down a busy city street or go to a large public occasion, I see a society at war with itself. Consequently, I am no longer puzzled as to why the world cannot make peace. To do so, we must first be at peace with ourselves.

At the conclusion of an interview with a leading magazine, the reporter said inquisitively, 'Can you see a stable relationship for me?' I looked into her eyes compassionately, and replied, 'Everlasting love magnetically seeks you, when you are ready and able to recognise and nurture it.' Unfortunately, her aura was so vulnerable and sensitive, I could only see a path of emotional entanglement. My heart wept for her and all of the other people I see with similar auras. We have analysed and carved up the very notion of relationships to form a multipurpose mould to suit any circumstance at any time that may be interpreted in any way by anybody. Is it then any wonder that more and more people are in search of peace of mind?

Relationships, as well as the personal patterns of behaviour that you have formed throughout your life, can easily be understood by consulting your aura. For a relationship to stand the test of time, it needs to be aurically compatible. To support you in this endeavour your subconscious mind reads all the data in an aura to stimulate your instincts. I have described a number of situations below where people relate to each other and what effect this has on their auras.

Haven't we met before?

When you meet someone for the first time you may instinctively feel that you have met them before, as your subconscious mind penetrates their auric field and recognises similarities or complementary feelings of expression. You may meet as adults and wonder how you instantly know each other, while your subconscious is clearly aware that as school children you occasionally stood beside each other while waiting for a train. Then, during discussion you both realise you grew up in the same town and travelled the same route, but to different schools.

I feel that I have known you all my life

Senses become alert as the subconscious mind instantly connects to the vital and astral layers of a person's aura, releasing an abundance of feelings which indicate that you have known this person all of your life. In this, like-mindedness is the key factor. The aura reveals a bond of friendship, learning and interest. As the relationship progresses you will discover that you have numerous things in common.

Love at first sight

The 'deep knowing' of the subconscious mind tugs at your heart strings and beckons you to form a relationship. Senses heighten and are overcome by passion. Time stands still, yet it passes by rapidly. All other aspects of life lose their importance. Nothing but this intense, connective yearning to be as one seems to matter. The mind becomes obsessive and possessive as the vital and astral layers of the auras merge.

Threads of auric energy form cord-like strands, securing the couple in love together. Over time the intense passion will fade into a mellow, contented bond which ensures their everlasting commitment to each other. Through the trials and tests of life, the ties will hold them firm. Such is the strength of these auric ties, that a couple will sometimes follow each other in death, in quick succession, either by natural causes or by suicide. As the ties begin to fade the individual's vital auric layer shrinks, rendering a feeling of life closing down, hence the phases of mourning.

Identical twins

When it comes to the human aura, identical twins are true individuals. The following illustration shows how the aura reflects each twin's attitudes and life experiences. While the twins will have an instinctive connection, giving rise to a tele-pathic link between them, only auric family connections will be similar. The thinking and feeling patterns of each twin set one apart from the other.

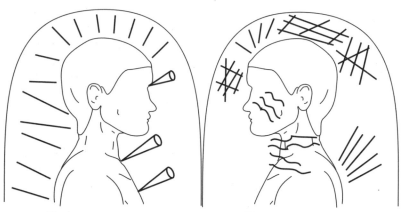

- Clear thinking
- Intuitively connected
- Caring, tolerant and charitable

- Frustrated and poor self-esteem
- Congested nasal and throat areas
- No sense of direction

They may look alike but the individuality of identical twins can be seen in their auras.

Lovemaking

In the loving thrusts of two bodies embracing, the auras merge to form one. Senses of the body that are aroused by love-making activate the physical, etheric, vital and astral auric layers which waste no time in taking the psyche to the highest of heights, enhancing the physical sensations. In the richness of love, feelings will be elated. In the sadness of love, feelings will be over-sensitised and exaggerated, leaving one, or both, of the partners with unfulfilled desires. In this circumstance, love-making becomes nothing more than physical gratification, because the two astral auric layers do not merge. Often when a person does not enjoy being touched or having sexual inter-course, there is an imbalance in the astral auric layer.

Childbirth

The aura of the mother merges with the unborn child at con-ception. As the foetus grows, it develops individual auric colours which determine its personality and state of health, although its aura is still strongly connected with the mother's aura. The developing foetus attunes its instincts to the emo-tions of the mother in order to communicate with the world into which it will be born.

At birth, the mother and child are forced to sever their physical tie and must go through the process of recognising and stimulating the replica umbilical cord within the etheric layer of the aura. When this is achieved, the perceptiveness of both mother and child to each other's needs is remarkable. A mother will wake up in the early hours of the morning just minutes before the baby awakens wanting to be fed. Should the mother be stressed by any emotional or financial circum-stances, her perceptiveness will wane. Hence perceptive com-munication between a mother and child in the first few weeks of life is extremely important and will determine their future relationship.

The father, who has lovingly spoken to and caressed the developing foetus in the womb, will be quick to connect to the etheric umbilical cord and establish a bond for life. It is this cord that unites family groups. However, should the father reject the child or its mother, the break in this tie may cause irreparable damage.

In the case of adoption, or when a child is placed in the long-term care of another person, the child will begin again the process of aurically bonding. However, each time a child is put in this position, the instinctive bonding nature of the astral aura will wither, thereby inhibiting the individual's ability to make a stable emotional commitment in adolescence and adulthood.

Separation and divorce

The intensity of the vital and astral layers of the aura can cause great discomfort when relationships attempt to untie the auric bond. The mind may logically justify the separation and the heart, in its frustration, may support the action. However, the aura is slow to process the events and steadfastly holds its links. Both partners will experience a heart-rending tug keeping them together, but often in different ways. The astral layer of the aura has grown used to linking the two individuals together, no matter what the distance. When a couple have been separated or divorced for some time the astral auric layer focuses its attention on self-development and relationships closer to home.

There is no better example of 'aurically letting go' than in the case of a conscientious mother who has to realise that her children have grown up and must be free to establish themselves in the world. Hence the popular saying 'untie the apron strings'. Her love does not dissipate, it merely reshapes itself and is redefined by her new role.

Sayings such as 'absence makes the heart grow fonder' and 'time heals all wounds' both describe the nature of the astral auric layer and its interaction within relationships.

DYNAMICS OF AN UNSUSTAINABLE RELATIONSHIP

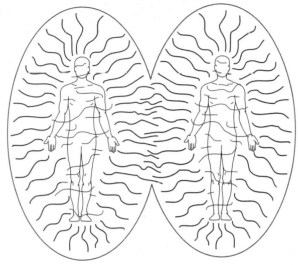

Two emotionally disturbed auras are attracted to each other because the similar patterns in their auras give rise to a sense of familarity.

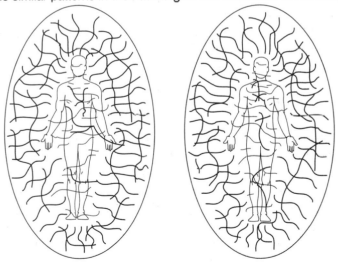

After a period of time the auras become intertwined with each other's frustration, creating imbalance and disillusionment, which ultimately means that the relationship will break down.

Friends and foes

No matter where you travel in the world you may strike up a friendship. That's the beauty of auras. The all-knowing etheric auric layer will always lead you to recognise like-minded people, especially when you are in need of support or direction. So many times I have heard the story of sightseers on a group holiday tour of a country. During the weeks they spend together, friendships form that may last for the remainder of their lives, supported by correspondence and visits to each other.

Contrary to this, what begins as a friendship can often turn into a painful experience. You only have to reflect on childhood experiences to realise just how often you have been exposed to gossip, rivalry and power ploys.

In the beginning of a relationship, the auras magnetically irradiate the charisma of the vital layer of the aura, thus attracting bees to the honey pot, so to speak. Then, as the astral aura of each individual combines, their strengths and weaknesses are sorted and sifted. However, in the emotional rush to be accepted, the mind overpowers the subconscious mind's instinctive awareness and an individual can fall blindly into a relationship that may cause them grief. At no stage in life is this more prevalent than during childhood and adolescence. Whereas once a person has developed a mature aura, the subconscious mind gleans what it needs to know cautiously, so as not to repeat painful patterns.

Why do I keep attracting people who hurt me?

If you find that you are attracting people who offend you, it means that your aura is running the wrong advertisement. Individuals with a lot of pale pink in their aura are vulnerable and often feel like everyone's doormat. Repeatedly, they are challenged and hurt because their emotional self dominates their reasoning, due to heightened sensitivity of the astral auric layer. Undertaking counselling or self-development courses can show immediate positive results.

While I was drawing the aura of a television celebrity, she asked me why 'Mr Right' had not come into her life. Examining her aura, I described the person which her friends and family saw in her. Then I described the person whom I saw beneath the veneer. The half-smile and the tear in her eye confirmed my findings. A fear of failing, together with a fear of being hurt, was definitely not the advertisement to lure 'Mr Right'. I suggested a change in the message that she was aurically giving out to the public at large. Firstly, to visualise welcoming a man who will complement her in every way and love her unconditionally. Secondly, to be happy in being who she is, a beautiful, creative and talented individual.

The human aura is immersed in the emotional web woven by the complex nature of ourselves, therefore making relationships an intregal part of the fabric of life. Choosing relationships that stimulate our thinking, support our emotions, encourage our personal development and enhance our spiritual enlightenment is vitally important, if we, as individuals and as a people, are to find true peace and fulfilment. The personal level of contentment is the product of auric balance and harmony.

3

SEEING AND PERCEIVING THE HUMAN AURA

If the fool would persist in his folly, he would become wise.

William Blake

In my earliest days of auric vision, I firmly believed that everyone had been touched by God. The pictures of Jesus Christ and his mother Mary, which hung in the corridors of my school and church, displayed the same gentle light which I saw around every person, animal and plant. As would be expected, their halos were somewhat brighter. I concluded that God had truly made mankind in his likeness, and had also blessed the world in which we live. In retrospect, it was a soothing concept, especially when, at times, peer group pressure threatened my belief in my God-given gift.

Everyone has the ability to see and read auras. It begins in childhood. In the first four weeks of life, you can only focus at about 25 centimetres, and during this time you are supported by your instincts and follow the contours of a person's aura with your eyes, interpreting it with your perception. During the first four weeks of life, the eyes are continuously going in and out of alignment as focus is developing. It's fascinating to watch a new baby tilt its head to the side and look at a person, not directly face on but at a slight side-angle.

Here, a mother in her mid-twenties delights in telling about her own experiences during her pregnancy. Kate is just one of the many new mothers-to-be to develop a greater awareness of their growing child through her understanding of the human aura.

Kate's story

When I was first pregnant I attended a three-day course run by Judith on 'Living the Life of Your Soul'. At that time, the news of my impending motherhood was still very new. I was overjoyed and overawed at the thought that we would be parents, but the reality of the person that was developing inside me had not struck me yet. I was still very much focused on the physical changes happening to my own body. Next to these tangible realities, the baby was still a fairly vague notion.

There was a long and detailed workshop on auras during this course. Judith knew about our baby, and perhaps for that reason, part of the discussion on auras had to do with the unborn child and pregnant mother. I listened, transfixed, as Judith described the faint life-force that first appears as a fragile light in the mother's aura. This light develops, deepening in luminescence and vividness as the baby grows inside the mother's womb.

Now I could see her and sense her presence—not as a tiny bundle of cells but as a pure and beautiful light, individual and unique, but in a special way connected to me. As my tummy bulged, I imagined the light of my daughter's aura growing. Pictures of the developing foetus made me think of the colours of her aura deepening like new eucalyptus leaves—from pale pink, to deep red, to green.

I was aware that she was also coming to identify the auras around her, and to associate the feel of those auras with the voices she heard. Whenever friends and relations reached out to touch my tummy, they thought they were feeling the baby, but I knew that in actual fact, she was feeling them! As they lay their palms over her, she could sense and interpret their auras through the energy emanating from their palms. At the same time, I could tell by the sparkle in their eyes and their glowing smiles that my baby was giving them a burst of her own pure energy.

We had a memorable taste of her ability to feel and recognise the auras of people around her on a visit to Judith when I was about seven months pregnant. As Judith rushed past me on her way to a client, she lightly touched my tummy and said, 'Hello Matija' to the baby. The baby's reaction was fantastic. She jumped and spun and kicked as if she had been given an electric shock. I could sense her joy and excitement at feeling Judith around her, and her impatience to be physically with us.

When she was born, my husband and I were always delighted to see her focusing on people's auras. We would watch her trace an outline of people's bodies, especially around their heads. This fascinated and entertained her. She really had no need to look directly at people, as she was recognising them by their auras, and associating the colours she saw with the feelings she'd felt before she was born. She started doing this immediately after her birth. In fact, Judith came to visit her when she was just hours old, and she actually opened her eyes, spun her head around and fixed her gaze at Judith's aura for minutes. The recognition was obvious.

Matija is one year old now, and she is a beautiful gift in our lives. I'm not sure whether she still actually sees the colours of the auras around her, but I know that she can sense them. She's an excellent judge of people, and seems to understand when people need the type of happy distraction that a baby can bring or, as her grandmother puts it, 'She's just so kind to people.' Understanding always brings compassion I guess.

A baby's vision develops rapidly in comparison with its body movements and coordination. Simple games like peek-a-boo aid in stimulating a child's focus. Around nine months old a child's eyes begin to see like that of an adult, but the child has yet to learn the meaning of what is being seen. Up to the age of approximately one to two years, a child is unable to independently recognise itself in a mirror—then dawn of learned recognition awakens. It is estimated that eighty per cent of a pre-school child's learning is done through vision.

During childhood the developing person has a view into tangible vision, combined with intuitive vision, which on reaching adulthood, has usually been long forgotten. This is because colourful vision is commonly discouraged and dismissed as 'childish' imagination by adults. Even worse, the child may visually and intuitively close down due to emotional abuse, separation and loss.

Although as an infant everyone sees auras, encouragement is rarely given to a child in order for them to comprehend and develop this ability. So, unfortunately, like many of the passing scenes witnessed daily by the eye, auric experiences are discounted as being irrelevant, and lodged in the subconscious mind's memory bank. Most adults must therefore start from scratch to learn again how to see auras.

Children who are encouraged, either in a small or large way, carry their auric insight into maturity. Some 'new age' parents pressure their children to constantly see auras and inadvertently force them to resort to make-believe. To preserve a child's auric vision a parent should listen to their child and support them but not lead them on in any way.

Sharon, a twelve-year-old girl, was brought to me by her mother. Sharon was reporting intimately detailed information about family friends and relatives to her mother within twenty minutes after the person had left the family home. The mother was beside herself—she didn't know what to think. Was her daughter prying? How did she get this information? The poor woman was both confused and deeply concerned. As Sharon sat opposite me, I could see myself in her at that age. An honest child, she reported her findings, not to gossip, but to share them with her mother, whom she felt would know what to do and how to help the friends and relatives.

I asked Sharon to close her eyes and tell me something about myself. With all the innocence of childhood she obeyed my command and within seconds told me of the personal trauma I had experienced at her age. I was impressed. I then asked her to open her eyes and look at me to see if she could add to the information she had already given. She glanced at the back and right side of my head and announced, 'Your grandmother, Margaret, is watching over you.' With that, I leaned forward and touched her hand. She pulled away when our combined aura went into overdrive, causing electric sparks to sting the finger tips.

There is no doubt in my mind that Sharon is one child who never lost her intuitive connection to life. Placing her under the guidance of a very dear spiritual friend of mine, who would help her to expand her comprehension, I felt confident that she would come to know the richness of her understanding, just as I have. To their credit, Sharon's parents are doing their utmost to grasp the world their daughter sees and hears, so that she is not branded as a freak, liar or misfit.

It is important that a child should be offered support, but in no way directed. Intuitive development opens for each and every one of us at the time appropriate to our learning. It is something that evolves at a pace to suit the individual, not the masses.

In 1992, while doing aura drawings at the Mind, Body and Spirit festival in Sydney, a five-year-old boy ran up to me and said, 'I can see all that.' I sat back for a minute to look at him. His mother pushed through the crowd that had gathered around me and said, 'Oh, he sees auras all the time. Tell Judith what her aura looks like.' And so, the child performed at the mother's command. His reading was totally inaccurate but I just smiled and waved him off. As the couple walked away, I experienced a heavy feeling in my heart because I could see that he had traded his intuitive instinct to act like a circus monkey, performing on call.

Feeling the aura

There are many ways every day that we touch and feel an aura, for example, shaking hands, cuddling, kissing, caressing, making love, or simply by jostling to get on a train or a bus. Even supermarket queues are amassed with people standing inside each other's auras. So, in short, it's no big deal. That is, until you understand what you are feeling.

Newly acquainted lovers feel with a different sense of touch. Their senses are heightened by the astral connection of their auras. Although they hold hands in the same way that a young child holds its mother's hand, the difference in what they are feeling alters their perception.

You attain an altered state of consciousness when you deeply relax. This hypersensitive state expands your awareness to a point where sounds seem louder, smells seem stronger, light and colours seem more vibrant and feelings are more acute. This is because relaxation amplifies your perceptive abilities and expands your awareness.

To feel your own aura, rub the palms of your hands together to activate the chakras. When you feel a tingling sensation, place one hand approximately two centimetres above the bend of your elbow, then close your eyes to attune to what you are feeling. The hand chakra should activate the minor chakra in the elbow, giving a warm, magnetic sensation.

Another way to feel your aura is to rub your hands together, and then place one hand approximately three centimetres above your head. Once again, close your eyes to attune to your feelings. The crown chakra should reveal its soft, bouncing-ball-like energy pulsating about the head.

Exercises

THE AURIC MINUET

This exercise helps to assess the strength and vibrance of your aura. You will need to find yourself a willing partner and set the scene with appropriate music to encourage your aura to dance the minuet.

1. Stand opposite each other, toe to toe, then take three average-sized steps backwards.
2. Close your eyes and stand with your feet comfortably apart. Take ten gentle, deep breaths to relax any muscular tension in your body. Focus your mind on your hands and facial skin as these areas will be first to detect the electro-magnetic rays of your partner's aura.
3. Take one step forward and attune to your senses once again. Allow your mind to seek out any variations in the feelings around your hands and face.
4. Take another step forward. At this stage your facial skin should be buzzing with the sensations of pin pricks as your auras sway to and fro. Allow your body to move freely. Don't be frightened of losing your balance. The magnetic pulling and thrusting you feel is simply your aura working at its normal pace. Be sure to set yourself a time limit so that you don't get sea sick!

On completion of this exercise, openly discuss what you discovered about each other. If compatible, your auras will pull together almost to the point of falling on top of each other. If you are incompatible, one or both auras will be uncomfortable, and want to pull away from the other. Incompatibility of auras usually occurs where one (or both) participant has a dominant personality.

ROMANCING THE AURA

This exercise stimulates the romantic senses by allowing you to slip inside each other's auras. As the electromagnetic particles magnify the sensations, the closeness of your combined energies gives off a feeling of inseparability, embracing love at its purest level.

1. Play some soft, melodic background music.
2. Lie opposite your loved one on the floor, your bare feet exactly four centimetres apart. Place your arms comfortably by your sides with the palms of your hands turned upwards. Place cushions under your knees and head for support and comfort.
3. Focus your attention on your feet. Feel their temperature. Feel the energy between your own and your partner's feet.
4. Take a deep breath, completely filling the lungs. Hold it for a slow count of three, then release the breath gently and slowly. Allow your breathing to return to normal.
5. Repeat step 4 five times. Then relax into a feeling of calmness and unity.

Within three to five minutes you will feel the pull of your auras as you are magnetically drawn together. Then an oscillating movement will become apparent to your senses. Enjoy this sensation, as it is the closest you can ever get to your loved one.

Determining your auric vision

Learning to regain your auric vision requires a commitment to both physical and metaphysical exercises. Many of the people whom I have taught over the years have been surprised at how quickly they respond to their desire to see and read the human aura. I advise that while you are grasping an understanding of auric colours and placements, you develop your eyesight to its fullest.

Before you begin any of the aura exercises in this book you need to understand how the language you use can turn your vision on and off. What you think, feel and say definitely plays a major role in your day-to-day life. The concept of positive thinking has been around for years. High achievers have had to believe in it, not only to overcome personal handicaps, but also because those of lesser vision have scorned their dreams and skills. Positive thinking encourages the mind to believe it has achieved its goal. 'I can see auras,' or, 'I know I see and perceive auras every day,' are two very positive phrases affirming your natural ability. Avoid using phrases such as, 'I've tried but I just can't see the aura,' or, 'I'm not intuitive enough to see the aura,' or, 'I must be a slow learner,' as such expressions lock into place patterns of self-doubt and set your learning back. Perseverance is the key word.

Exercise

DISCOVER YOUR LEVEL OF INTUITIVENESS
By completing the following exercise, you can determine how, during your life, you have perceived the aura of another person. You will soon discover your level of intuitiveness. Place the number one [1] in the boxes when you answer yes to a question, then total your score.

[ ]   Have you ever experienced an instant dislike for a person?
[ ]   Have you ever met a person and felt as if you have known them all of your life?
[ ]   Have you ever walked into an empty room and immediately felt uneasy?
[ ]   Have you telephoned a friend or relative, believing them to be in need of you, and they were?
[ ]   Have you ever sensed a person's presence minutes or hours before physically seeing them?
[ ]   Have you felt the phone was going to ring moments before it did?
[ ]   Do certain individual colours or colour combinations excite or depress you?
[ ]   Have you experienced a first impression of a person which turned out to be right?
[ ]   Have you known how someone was feeling as they tried to hide it from you?
[ ]   Have you ever felt a person staring right through you?
[ ]   Have you ever met a person who made a lasting impression on you?

[   ]   Have you ever known what someone was thinking moments before they said it?

[   ]   Have you experienced love-at-first-sight?

[   ]   Are animals readily attracted to you?

[   ]   Do your gut feelings often turn out to be correct?

How did you score?

(1–5) Explore your own creativity to help you to open your perception of the world around you. You are a true beginner but don't feel downhearted. With dedication and practice you will reopen your auric sight.

(6–9) With ongoing practice, the exercises in this book will enhance your intuition and open your auric vision.

(10–15) You are ready to develop auric vision. Practise the exercises in this book and watch yourself excel.

To interpret an aura accurately you must fully develop your perception. Telepathy is one aspect of perception and intuitiveness the other. By answering the questions in the exercise above, you have determined the level of your perceptive experience to date. Whomever you meet, wherever you go, your subconscious mind reads all the data in auric fields. An instant dislike of a person is a warning that you are open to be emotionally hurt by them. An uneasy feeling in an empty room is an indication of a disruptive influence, lingering on from those who last inhabited it. A repulsion or excitement to certain colours indicates a colourful emotional memory tied to a past experience. Therefore each time your eyes see the colour you respond physically and/or emotionally.

Our instinctive telepathic ability can be triggered by vulnerability, excitement or peace of mind, depending on personality types. For example, clairvoyant phenomena may occur for one person during meditation, for another during a daydream state and for another while in a dramatic dancing or chanting frenzy. Most people think of telepathic ability as being unique to psychics, when in fact is it the very essence of our communication. Everyone's life is filled with telepathic encounters, which are generally mistakenly called coincidence.

A young mother may wake up in the early hours of the morning thinking that her baby is crying, only to find the baby isn't. Then as she dozes back off to sleep, the baby awakens crying for her attention. Here, the mother's bond to her child exhibits the intuitive communication link.

A man was travelling to work when his car broke down. For the first time, his son decided not to catch the train but to drive to work. Something in his mind suggested that he take a different route. Consequently he met up with his father and was able to tow the broken down vehicle to the nearest garage. (See also 'The telepathic aura' on page 83.)

Your level of perceptiveness depends on an inner strength that is solely fed by self-acceptance.

The language and feelings of auric vision

Emotional turmoil can stunt learning and a demanding job can drain the mind's creative juices. To ensure clarity of auric vision you need to keep on top of life. Scan the left-hand column in the table below to find the words that currently describe an aspect of yourself and then refer to their counterparts in the right-hand column to see what you need to do in order to correct any imbalances, or to maintain balance, for awakened auric sight and perception.

Obscured sight	Awakened sight
Tense	Be keen
Frightened	Feel secure
Distracted	Be focused
Despairing	Be expansive
Constrained	Come alive

Obscured sight	Awakened sight
Scattered	Become connected
Unhappy	Be joyful
Empty	Be fulfilled
Hopeless	Be faithful
Rigid	Be perceptive
Hoping	Inner knowing

Seeing the aura

What is now proved was once only imagin'd.

William Blake

It doesn't take courage and it doesn't take mind power to see an aura. All it takes is relaxation, intuitive focus and the knowledge that you are simply re-awakening an instinctive ability that has been asleep for years. Be prepared to try, try and try again, and don't be discouraged easily.

Each exercise you undertake brings you one step closer to opening yourself to a new dimension of life. Even today, I still discover things I have never seen before. Just think of the benefits that seeing and reading auras will bring to your life and how much richer in character you will be once the conscious and intuitive minds begin to work as one. It can be great fun.

One night, following a heavy day's work while I was on a lecture tour in Western Australia, I flopped in front of the television, beckoning it to divert my focus. It did just that. An enthralling movie of entangled relationships and mystery had just begun. My husband cuddled close beside me and we both relaxed into viewing. After an hour, I felt myself growing exceedingly sleepy. I could barely keep awake. The television had obviously done its job of diverting my thoughts. I read the auras of the main actors because they know the script, and then explained the outcome of the plot to my husband, who, in turn, rebelliously sat through the entire movie to check my findings. In the light of the morning he concurred with me and was tired by his vigilance.

Seeing auras is not confined to person-to-person viewing. When you master your auric vision you will be able to see the emanations in colour photographs, television and cinema as all these frequencies capture colour auric vibrations.

In the beginning, you can expect to see only the physical and etheric layers as a faint milky white or blue haze about the head, shoulders, feet or hands. As the mind, over a period of time, accepts the experience as being real, the beautiful, transparent colours of the vital and astral auric layers will reveal themselves to you. There is no set time period or limit to developing auric sight. One person's response will be quicker than another's.

Remember at all times that you are a unique individual and therefore should not compare yourself to others.

The eye

The retina, which lines the back of the eye, is made up of cones and rods which perceive information about light and colour. They transmit electrochemical signals that travel along optic nerves to other nerve pathways. It is generally thought that light of a specific wavelength (i.e. colour) is analysed by the cones.

There are three types of cones, each with a particular sensitivity to the primary colours blue, green and red. Sensitivity of the individual cone types is not limited to only the one light wavelength. Cones for green light are also sensitive to blue light. This can cause the observer great confusion (see 'Colour blindness' on page 74 All other colours we see are a combination of these primary colours.

The eye works to convert the light coming from the outside environment into an electrical message that the brain can process as sight. The iris, a muscle of the eye, opens and closes to govern the amount of light the eye receives. The lens then changes shape to focus on what you are looking at.

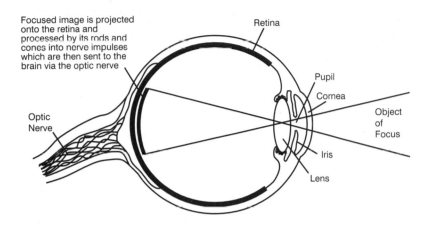

Focused image is projected onto the retina and processed by its rods and cones into nerve impulses which are then sent to the brain via the optic nerve

Retina

Pupil

Cornea

Object of Focus

Optic Nerve

Iris

Lens

CROSS-SECTION OF THE EYE

How the eye sees auras

When the rods and cones of the eyes colour attune, they can clearly capture the oscillating colour auric vibrations through the normal process of vision (see the colour stimulation exercise opposite page 97). However, what is seen is not interpreted +with logical thought but with the thoughts and feelings of the sixth sense—your intuitive self. You are instantly made aware that what you are seeing is different to natural light vibrations. This is why the development of your perception together with good eyesight is of paramount importance in seeing auras.

During my aura courses, I have found that most people who wear glasses see auras better without their glasses. I believe this is because glasses are specifically designed to correct focus and auric emanations are slightly out of focus. So, please do try it, you might be in for a big surprise.

Colour blindness

According to popular belief, one in every two hundred women and one in every twenty-five men are colour blind (i.e. have defective colour vision). It is thought to be a hereditary condition passed on from mother to son. It may be due to a lack of the cone types associated with one or more of the primary colours. This causes confusion when a person is interpreting colour variations, the most common being red and green.

It is wise to note that colour blindness is not always a hereditary condition and can come about at any time during a person's life as a result of vitamin deficiency, disease or exposure to toxic substances. However, colour blindness should not prevent a person from developing the skills of reading auras. On its own, the intuitive perception necessary to interpret an aura accurately will suffice. Those born blind must rely on their intuitive perception and instincts to survive the challenges of life. In fact, they become so attuned that a skilled blind person can feel the vibration of a colour and identify it accurately.

Illusions of sight

The eyes are both an asset and a handicap when learning to see auras because reality isn't always what it seems. To understand how illusions can confuse the novice aura observer, we need to look at how we perceive colour. Worldwide, people have learnt how to make the optical illusion of colour work for them. Dark colours and vertical stripes make the body look slimmer. White buildings look larger than those of darker tones. These are perfect examples of how both the eye and the brain can be deceived.

Scenes, too, are not always how and what the eyes see. For example, when you drive along a country road and look into the car's rear vision mirror, your eyes would have you believe that the further away you go, the smaller the road and the trees and shrubs that line it become. As the lenses of the eyes adjust their focus, the eyes report images in dwarf size. It's our learned perception that assures us we are not living in a world of midgets and giants. So, while development of the eyes assists you in visually seeing the aura, your perception will determine what is an illusion and what is not.

Lighting conditions for seeing auras

To see an aura the human eye requires light (or at night, moonlight). Direct sunlight and fluorescent light can obscure auric vision because the intense light dominates the bright, yet subtle auric emanations. For the beginner, soft lamp or candlelight allows the eye to detect an aura more easily. Moonlight creates the perfect auric viewing conditions. Let me share with you a number of personal incidents which have been helped by auric viewing on a moonlit evening.

I live on a small property, nestled in an isolated, wooded area. We are without street lights, so, when we arrive home from an evening out, moonlight is our natural torch. When it's a full moon, we can easily find our way to the front door. However, during the other phases of the moon when the natural light is poor, the human eye is dimmed by night vision, especially under the canopy of tall trees. Fortunately, one of our cats regularly rushes to greet us. As we alight from the car, the cat makes his way to the front verandah and I simply follow his aura. Most of the time he leads us directly to the front door, but on occasions I've ended up in the garden bed!

About fifteen years ago some teenagers went on the rampage and stoned several houses in the street in which we were then living. For over an hour a handful of police tried to catch them, but to no avail. Growing tired of the three-hour escapade, my husband suggested that every house be asked to turn off their outdoor and indoor lights in the hope that the gang would come out of their random hiding places. Our house looked down the street, so every house was visible. As the boys in hiding moved from shrub to shrub, I could see their auras and within an hour the police had caught them all.

One night my pet rabbit, who lives in a very comfortable cage in line with the bay window of my bedroom, was frantically racing around her cage. My husband crawled out of bed to see what the commotion was about. In the darkness of the early hours of the morning, he could not see anything. When I pulled back the curtain to locate her aura, I saw the aura of two other animals. It was a young fox and his mother, who was teaching him the tricks of the trade. Bugsey, my rabbit, knew that she was safe and was darting back and forth teasing their appetites.

For me, it's awe-inspiring to walk around my property in the warm, dark, stillness of a summer's night and see the subtle auric colours silhouetting cows, horses and goats as they quietly graze among the auric glow of the trees.

Exercises

CENTERING PERCEPTION AND VISON

This simple and quick technique is a preparatory exercise for aligning intuitive perception and vision for aura readings.

1. Close your eyes and sit perfectly still and quiet for a few moments to allow the aura to process the adjustment.
2. Inhale a deep breath slowly through your nose.
3. Hold the breath and look for tension in the mind and body.
4. Expel tension with a quick exhale of the breath through the mouth.
5. Do this three times. Then, allow the breath to return to normal.

This exercise should leave you feeling at ease, because the pressures of mind and body tension have shifted.

ATTUNING THE EYE'S FOCUS TO MOVING ENERGY PATTERNS

This exercise will help the eye recognise shifting and pulsating colours in an energy field.

1. Position a lighted candle in front of you in a darkened room.
2. Concentrate your focus on the energy pattern of the aura around

the flame for approximately three to five minutes.

3. Close and rest the eyes for a few seconds.

Be careful not to overdo this exercise. If you should feel pressure at the back of the eyes or the forehead, it's your body's way of telling you to go gently and slowly.

STRENGTHENING AND CO-ORDINATING THE EYES

The eyes view objects, both near and far, in spirals. This causes the eye muscles to alter the shape of the lens so that the object of your attention will come into the focus of the retina. This exercise encourages both eyes to work together, which will strengthen your depth of vision.

1. Focus on the central core of the spiral which should take on a cave-like appearance.
2. Close your eyes and rest them for a few moments.
3. Slowly bring your focus out of the centre by viewing each line in the spiral, one at a time.
4. Repeat this pattern of viewing.
5. Practise this exercise daily for three to five minutes and you will be able to pull your vision in and out.

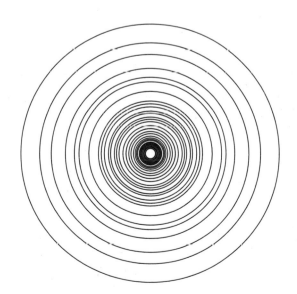

LAYER PENETRATION

This exercise enhances the eyes' ability to penetrate the layers of the aura, as well as the overlaying patterns in the aura that form as a result of emotional imbalance and ill-health.

1. Focus your eyes on the centre of the triangle for approximately one minute.
2. Close your eyes for one minute to relax the eye muscles.
3. Follow this procedure for ten minutes.

Each time you focus on the centre of the triangle you should experience an increased sense of depth and penetration of the close-knit layers.

FLEXIBLE EYE MOVEMENT

This exercise stimulates the rods and cones of the retina. By moving your eyes in quick succession you will develop their ability to quickly recognise shapes, tone and light.

1. Cover one eye and focus on any one of the eight points.
2. Quickly move your eye to an opposite point, then sweep it back to your starting point.
3. Move your eye from point to point using circular, vertical, horizontal and diagonal movements for about twenty seconds.
4. Cover your other eye and repeat these steps, then repeat the exercise using both eyes.
5. Continue this sequence for one or two minutes.

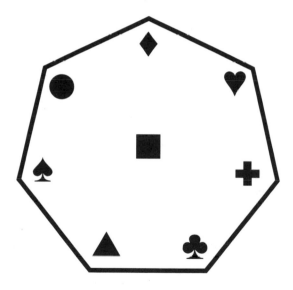

If you experience eye strain while doing this exercise, stop and close both eyes to rest them. Often when the eye muscles have been lazy or dormant, you will feel strain and should gradually build up the time spent doing this exercise.

SEEING YOUR OWN AURA

I've lost count as to the number of times that I have been asked if I can see my own aura, and how I do it. The technique is quite easy. Most bathrooms are decorated in pastel shades with a large mirror, and are therefore suited to seeing your own aura. If this description fits your bathroom, then you have the perfect place for self-viewing.

1. Stand in front of a large mirror with your feet comfortably apart for balance.
2. Close your eyes and take two or three gentle, deep breaths to relax your body muscles.
3. Open and close your eyes several times to help them break the staring focus, and look into the mirror to see the auric outline reflected on the wall behind you.

I have a full-length mirror on my bathroom door just for this purpose.

SEEING AURIC HANDS

This is an easy exercise for beginners. Your hands radiate and receive energy. Therefore, the auric emanations are very strong, making your hands the easiest part of the body for aura viewing. However, you need to set the right atmosphere.

1. Use low-light conditions: a corner lamp is suitable.
2. Hold your hand at arm's length against a white backdrop.
3. After a while, get closer to your hand—bring it to approximately twenty-five centimetres from your face.
4. Look carefully between the fingers and at the fingertips.
5. You may see a thin band of whitish, pale blue or a blue-grey colour immediately next to the skin.

By practising this exercise regularly, not only are you encouraging the mind's acceptance, you are expanding your ability to see auras. The subtle auric emanations will expand to reveal a depth of colour.

ADVANCED AURA VIEWING

When you advance to this exercise, your choice of partner is of paramount importance. Firstly, you should feel totally at ease with the person.

Secondly, he or she should have no expectations of you, to avoid the fulfilment of mindful imagination which will block the flow of intuitive vision. The person should be dressed in non-patterned, bland coloured clothing: fawn, beige, white or pale grey are the most suitable colours. Remember to move your eyes gently and quickly and under no circumstance stare, as this may change the focus of your eyes. Now you are ready for action.

1. Choose a relaxing thirty minute piece of music. This takes the hard edge off the silence and lowers the tension of anticipation by both you and your partner.
2. Dim the lights slightly to remove the harshness of bright light and to encourage auric light to open itself to you. A corner lamp is most suitable. Don't be tempted to use candlelight as the flickering flame will distract the eyes and cause the light to waver.
3. Ask your partner to close their eyes and contemplate relaxing thoughts by visually creating a tranquil scene in their mind.
4. Close your eyes and focus on your breath, encouraging it to quieten the heart and the stomach muscles and to reach a point of relaxation of focus. Partially open your eyes, then close them gently, allowing them to rest closed for a few seconds. Repeat this pattern five times, to break the normal focal routine of your eyes.
5. Partially open your eyes gently and slowly. Look to the side of the head of your partner for the thin whitish-blue layer of the physical aura. Then close and rest your eyes.
6. Again, partially open your eyes. Follow the contours of your partner's body in search of the whitish-blue layer of the physical aura.
7. Scan across the forehead from left to right and then right to left.
8. Gently allow your focus to drop to chest level and scan across the body, back and forth. Follow this system until you have scanned the entire body.

If you are unable to pick up any light or colour, relax the eyes and then move the eyes in quick succession horizontally, diagonally, vertically and in a circular motion. If you capture fleeting colour don't discard it, but close your eyes and hold it in your memory. Until you are used to holding the subtle auric vibrations in your mind, colour may move rapidly in and out of view.

As you become proficient in locating the physical layer of the aura, the etheric layer will become easier to see. And, once you have mastered these two layers, your eyesight should have advanced enough to see the vivid colours of the vital layer. Remember, at all times, that regaining your natural auric vision is not necessarily going to be a spontaneous process. So do, try, try and try again.

GROUP SIMULATION

One of the easiest ways to detect the subtle physical auric layer is via group focus. Organise a group of friends to sit closely in a circle in a dimly lit room. The chairs should be almost touching, and each person should rest their palms on the palms of their neighbours' hands, that is left palm up, and right palm down. Elbows should be comfortably bent and not stretched out tightly, as this causes shoulders and arms to ache during the exercise.

1. Each person is to close their eyes and focus on their spine to make certain that it is comfortable. If not, gently move about until your posture is correct.
2. Take a deep breath slowly through the nose. Hold it for the count of three and then release the breath as slowly as you can through the mouth. This encourages the body to relax. Do this five times, then allow the breath to return to normal.
3. Open your eyes and look to the side of the hairline of the person sitting opposite you. Then close your eyes.
4. Open, look and close your eyes. Do this ten times, slowly.
5. Open, look and close your eyes in very quick succession—as fast as you normally blink. Do this five times.
6. Open your eyes and look at the hairline of the person opposite you, tracing it from shoulder to shoulder.

At first you will see the subtle light of the aura. However, if the group does this exercise two more times, the auric emanations will deepen in colour.

Those who wear glasses should try the exercise with and without them, to determine the best focus.

The telepathic aura

The aura's electromagnetic force field blends quite readily with the earth's atmosphere, communicating and living via it, and creating a complex and highly charged auric web. In a family, auras interchange to give and take what is necessary to align with each other, and in the process, form a unique family aura. This enlarged aura expands through the ceiling, and a little beyond the rooftop of a single-storey building. On reaching this height it links with neighbouring family auras and forms a communal aura, which, in turn, connects with the whole town as well as other towns and cities to form a social aura, which ultimately becomes the collective consciousness of a society. This atmospheric connection allows thoughts and feelings to connect to air waves and be carried along both far and near to merge with other social auras to create a complex global aura, which allows people to communicate telepathically.

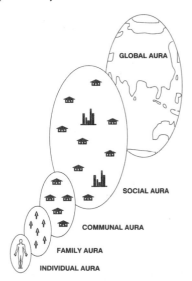

THE AURIC WORLD

Let me demonstrate the telepathic auric 'hotline' communication service via the global aura by recounting a story shared with me by a client. She and her brother had saved long and hard to travel in Europe and planned to backpack their way to minimise the cost. To their surprise a family friend who lived in England offered them his vacant apartment in London for the British leg of their tour.

They travelled through the Swiss Alps, Belgium, Austria, and on to Germany before going their separate ways for two weeks. He stayed to explore Germany further and she went on to London. Ten minutes after arriving at Gatwick airport a man knocked her to the ground and ran off with all her personal belongings. She was left shocked and dumbfounded, with only the clothes she stood in, plus the key to the apartment, linked securely to a chain around her neck.

Dazed and walking aimlessly along a crowded street she met a policeman who was quick to respond to her temporary destitution. She arrived at the apartment, hungry and tired, and threw herself onto the bed and cried herself to sleep. The shock and exhaustion had taken its toll on her travel-worn body, causing her to sleep deeply until 11 a.m. the following day. She woke to a hard, firm knock rattling the front door. Fearful of who it might be, she sat quietly and didn't respond. A familiar voice shouted out her name. It was her brother. He had been plagued with a feeling that all was not well and so had cancelled his plans and come to her aid.

Perceiving auric energy through the telephone

Fans of the Ron Edwards' programme on Radio 6PR in Perth, Australia, have become aware of just how easy it is for me to attune myself to the atmospheric waves of the social aura, and use a telephone as the go-between. The first word the caller utters establishes their auric patterns within my inner vision. This is because the voice creates its own patterns in an aura, thus personalising it. I don't need to engage in discussion at all. Immediately my mind has a clear vision of the person's auric colours and health.

Ernie, a casual listener to the programme, called on his mobile phone while in transit. Ron welcomed him to the show. But before Ernie had the chance to utter one word to me, I enquired as to what he had done to his right thumb, as aurically I saw it as swollen and painful. I went on to explain that a foreign object was deeply lodged in the wound, poisoning it. Ernie reported that he had bathed it and applied several different recommended ointments, but that nothing seemed to help. I suggested he consult his doctor immediately. Needless to say, Ron Edwards was speechless, and the producer of the show was staring at me with amazement. Ernie contacted Ron some time later to report his doctor's findings of a small piece of rose thorn which had caused the wound to turn septic.

Atmospheric global waves break distance barriers causing aura readings to be localised no matter how far the reader and the client are apart. The first time Ron Edwards interviewed me was via the telephone. He was in Western Australia and I was in New South Wales. At the conclusion of the interview I described a mole on his body which looked to me as if it required serious attention, and suggested that I look at it on my arrival in Perth in three weeks time. However, Ron decided to take no chances and sought his doctor's advice, who, drawing the same conclusion as me, removed the mole.

When you are next engaged in a telephone conversation, test your telepathic skills in perceiving the aura. Close your eyes while speaking to avoid distraction. Listen to the conversation with your feelings. Look for images or patterns in your mind. Colours and symbols may flash in and out of focus. When the conversation is complete, immediately write down your findings in an orderly way so that you can begin to understand what you have experienced.

The skill of reading auras through the telephone is of great value to counselling services, as well as big business.

Aura photography

The invention of aura cameras has taken the New Age movement by storm. Now at every fair, you can see people lining up eager to have their aura photographed. People, sceptical of how electronic equipment could capture the human aura, frequently ask me if the process is accurate and how it works. I have invited a well-known, successful team who work in this field to explain the function of the equipment. Joe Summers and Elizabeth Jansen of Aura Vision International work with one of the originally patented aura cameras.

> The spectrophotometer box contains a high speed digital computer controller and program to automate the aura recording process, special circuits to measure the electromagnetic interactions and optical signal processors.
>
> The computer controller incorporates a microprocessor with sixteen bit architecture for near instanteous performance. Special input circuits measure electromagnetic interaction with a person to detect the aura. Energy is transferred through the circuit and is converted to a voltage that approaches a steady state value. Data from the input circuits is modified by a spectrophotometric program contained in the computer and sent to the optical signal processors and to the camera.
>
> The aura camera contains high quality optics, shutter, Polaroid film holder and optical signal converters. The optical signal converters transfer data from the input circuits, as modified by the spectrophotometer program, and transfer the aura image to the film, along with the image of the person, to produce a colour photograph of the person and the aura.

Aware of their concerted effort to ensure quality and accuracy, I employed Joe's and Elizabeth's professional services to photograph my aura for this book. Joe, a respected Reiki Master (healer), and Elizabeth, a gentle lady endowed with acute intuitive awareness, set about organising me to pose for the aura portraits opposite page 96. Seated, I placed one hand on a black box which recorded my auric vibrations through an electrical current as Joe clicked the camera shutter. Each photograph depicts the focus of the mind. Taken approximately ten minutes apart, one can easily see how quickly the aura around the head changes with the mind's focus.

Colour aura images display a wide selection of varying energies depending on the quality of the equipment. The addition of computer analysis has brought the aura into the 'hightech' realm, giving it a sophisticated persona. To my disappointment, cheaper cameras which produce poor quality results have invaded the market. It's sad, but in some areas aura photography has simply become the 'cash crop' of the New Age.

The responsibility of auric vision

A huge responsibility rests with you when you can see and read the human aura, so you need to temper the ability with diplomacy and counselling skills. People feel threatened when they know that a person can read their aura, so you have to be very careful not to betray their trust or embarrass them.

Some years ago, when I was working at a festival, a young woman ushered a middle-aged woman towards me to draw her aura. As I glanced at the aura I saw the warning signs across her heart. I drew her close to me and raised questions about the condition of her health and she informed me that she was on medication but she couldn't be bothered taking it because she couldn't understand all the fuss. I pleaded with her to take her doctor's advice. Taking the aura drawing from me she aggressively pushed it into her handbag and stormed off into the crowd. I called to the young woman who was unaware that her friend had left.

As luck would have it she turned out to be the woman's eldest daughter. I informed her of my findings and watched the shock change the skin tone of her face. She stood very still and then ushered a middle-aged man towards me. As I glanced at his aura, it revealed recent heart surgery. On completion of his aura, the young woman came forward and said, 'Dad, did you know that mum has a serious heart problem and is on medication from a heart specialist? Judith just discovered it.' His mouth dropped as his breath quickened. Fixing his gaze on me he said, 'Nothing she does would surprise me. Did you know that we have been married for thirty-five years and in all that time she has told me nothing about herself. Sad isn't it. But, I've done my best.' I wished them both well as they walked away. I knew that I had opened Pandora's Box. No wonder the woman stared daggers at me when I uncovered her secret.

I pride myself on protecting the privacy and rights of people. So it took me days of analysing the situation to realise what I did was right.

In a second incident, while I was drawing the aura of a man in his late seventies, I discovered advanced patterns of cancer. I could see scar tissue where previous cancerous growths had been removed, so I decided to approach him with my findings. To my surprise as I began to speak, he placed his hand on my shoulder and said, 'I know what you are going to say, the cancer has come back. You know, I just can't face any more treatment. I'm too tired and too old.' I assured him of his right to choose his own reality. A year later, an elderly woman friend of his came to see me. She explained how he had died in peace and wanted me to know that I had reduced his suffering by allowing him the right to die. Still, today, the sincerity of this brings tears to my eyes.

As I have grown up with auric sight, intuitive counselling is now second nature to me. However, in my developing years I put myself on the line several times by innocently giving my findings to people who either didn't care to know, or were embarrassed by my knowing. Even now, at times my friends and family are uncomfortable in my presence, because they have come to recognise the auric look my eyes take on when I am reading and hearing them at the same time. A very dear friend summed it up when he said, 'Considering you can see me warts and all, I must have something special to be counted as one of your friends.'

I have had to learn to develop ethical guidelines for auric vision. This is the code by which I live:

- During a general conversation respond to what is being spoken about, not what you are seeing aurically.
- Allow a person to tell you how they feel by listening to them, not by reading their aura.
- Personalities are often protective barriers for emotions, i.e. the extrovert may really be an introvert.
- People are unique in their energy vibrations; blossoming at their own time and at their own pace.
- Auric vision should be treated as a non-invasive, non-violent, non-aggressive, non-judgemental tool.
- Everyone has a right to personal dignity.
- My ability is a service to others.

However, at times my ethics become a double-edged sword when I hear friends cry out, 'Why didn't you say? You knew all the time didn't you?' or 'You know more than you are revealing. What aren't you telling me?' Sometimes, I just can't satisfy anyone!

I am always disappointed when I come across other intuitively aware people who do not show any respect for the privacy of others. I recall one such incident. A clairvoyant walked up to a colleague of mine, who is well known in the lecture circuit, and said in a loud, determined voice in front of thirty people, 'I can see you have marriage problems. Oh, a custody battle I think. Whatever is going on, it looks pretty messy. You poor thing. It's damaging your relationship with your kids you know and giving you some back trouble.' At this point I wanted to take off my shoe and throw it at the clairvoyant.

My colleague didn't know where to look or what to say after this dramatic outburst. My quick wit tossed a throwaway line into the emotionally charged arena and everyone laughed. With the atmosphere broken, I ushered my colleague into a private place to regain her composure. The clairvoyant was correct in her analysis.

I feel it shows poor character when someone attempts to prove their skills in public at someone else's expense.

4

COLOUR IN THE AURA

The pride of the peacock is the glory of God.

William Blake

Since childhood, colour has been the greatest fascination of my life. My young eyes captured the beauty and joy of nature. The way that light produces shades of colour and springs from leaf to leaf in a garden. The glowing halo around the head of every person I met led me in my early years to believe that everyone was indeed holy!

As I grew up, my mother taught me to distinguish colours; red from crimson, purple from violet, magenta from indigo and so on. Although I was tutored in the art of identifying colours, their meaning and specific value in the aura was not always clear to me. It was only through experience that I learnt how to interpret the placement and combinations of colours in the aura. By my late teens I was thoroughly aware of the positive and negative attributes of colour in the aura, and I could accurately read an aura at great distance—not always to the delight of my friends! Playfully, I would bet a small sum of money and have them guess who was coming down the road towards us. To them, the figure was a mere blur. To me it was as clear as crystal. None of my friends ever believed how I managed to win their money. Nevertheless, they quickly gave up playing that game with me.

Colour is a part of everyday language as we can see in these commonly used terms: red with rage, got the blues, yellow streak, green with envy, blacked out, baby pink, and your bank account is either in the red or in the black.

Interestingly, the colours that people see today were not seen by our ancestors according to historians and researchers. It seems that as the intellect develops within a society, colour vision expands, giving the eyes more power. One wonders if the fast pace of modern society is a contributory factor as to why so many people are wearing glasses nowadays.

Auric colours and what they mean

Although many people see auras from time to time, very few know how to interpret them accurately because a working knowledge of auric colour is essential. I have come to learn that every colour seen in an aura has a strong influence on the aura, but that each colour's strength differs from that of any other colour due to their different wavelengths and auric frequencies.

Auric colours represent life and liberate an individual from black and white thinking and feelings. As people, we are limited by our ability to only see a few colours between violet and red in the colour spectrum. Either side of red or violet, there are a number of colours so bright and so wonderful that our physical eyes would be blinded by their radiance. I am amazed at how many new shades of colour have entered my auric sight over the past ten years. I believe that as we each spiritually evolve, our conscious world expands to see colours we have never seen before, hear sounds we have never heard, and embrace new thoughts.

Here in my presentation of auric colours, my lifetime's learning reveals the tried and tested theories gleaned from the personal experiences of the thousands of people who have crossed my path for over forty years. Expand and revitalise your world through understanding auric colours.

AQUA

Aqua denotes a healing teacher or empowered healing skills. Therefore it is not commonly seen in an aura. Its presence is due to a person's natural God-given talents or from skilled training.

BLACK

Black in the aura plays many roles. It is a defensive vibration when you are fearful of others or, adversely, portrays secretive behaviour. It is the absence of light in black which unfortunately prohibits appropriate support and guidance, and it is therefore often seen in the auras of abused children, divorcees, torture victims, refugees, and drug abusers. When black appears in various layers of the aura, it can indicate damage to either the emotions, self-esteem or organs. Black's aggressive energy spreads through the aura, steadily absorbing its radiance of colour and stifling its life-force. When it is seen with splashes of crimson, it's an indicator of intense evil, of the most vicious kind—the type of person you wouldn't want to meet down a dark alley.

BLUE

Pale blue is the colour of sensitivity. It shows a heightening of emotions and imagination. Too much of it can indicate a struggle towards maturity. In an artist, writer, actor or interior decorator pale blue is combined with orange or red which usually suggests that they are attuned, via their emotions, to the world around them. However, for most of the population pale blue energy usually represents a melodramatic personality or one who is too open to the opinion of others. Headaches and heartaches are associated with this colour.

Sky blue shows a strong 'gut instinct' perceptiveness. This intuition, although strong, is not consciously recognised as psychic power by the individual.

Cobalt blue depicts pure intuition emanating from the higher mental level of the aura. When in the aura the person is intuitively fortunate, gathering together resources to help them in all aspects of their life. For instance, purchasing a block of land and then discovering it contains the country's finest resource of mineral water.

Prussian blue represents a harmonious nature, good fortune as well as an expansion of the feminine aspect. When seen around the feet it wards off auric invasion to ensure a smooth reality.

Royal blue indicates that the person has found their chosen path. It further represents good judgement and honesty. It stimulates and expands the skills of those working in health care professions.

Delft blue denotes a steadfast character with an ethical approach to all aspects of life, love and work. When seen around the head and hands it may indicate wisdom and saintliness. However, in abundance it can impede natural instinctive and logical decision-making skills because the person is weighed down with ethics. When seen near or around the feet, a person may be re-evaluating their goals.

Ultramarine is most commonly seen in the aura around the hands of fishermen, sailors and surfers, because it connects human auric vibrations with the vibrations of the sea.

Navy blue indicates an evaluation of ethics and when seen anywhere in the aura can cause the person to make slow, but safe, progress.

Indigo is the colour of psychic abilities. It presents itself around the head and the hands. When teamed with white it shows that the person also has telepathic abilities. The auras of famous clairvoyants and mediums, such as Doris Stokes, are usually cloaked in indigo.

BROWN

Amber indicates a reinforcement of personal strength or new found courage to confront a challenge, and is commonly found in the auras of people applying for a new job or promotion, returning to the workforce after many years of absence, or someone making their acting, singing or public speaking debut.

Often when you wish a person good luck, you are subconsciously recognising the colour of amber in their aura.

Caramel is the colour of enthusiasm for a practical, sensible project. Those renovating or extending their homes or advancing their career, usually have the colour caramel draped around their shoulder and arm area.

Copper indicates a deep association with the earth's minerals. I have never seen it in the auras of city dwellers, only those who are involved in mine prospecting.

Raw sienna (a yellowish brown) has a muddying affect on the aura and may indicate physical discomfort due to poor decision-making. If the colour is around the head, the person is unable to think clearly. If it is under, or around, the feet, the person will feel bogged down.

Fawn means that a period of confusion is coming to an end. The person can expect to progressively regain their confidence and clarity of thought.

Doe-skin indicates a practical nature, with self-planning and self-governing being strong factors in the person's day-to-day life. The mind keeps an orderly system.

Mushroom represents a slowing of destiny. A person with mushroom around their hands or feet will feel that no matter how hard they try, life just doesn't move as fast as they would like it to.

Chocolate brown shows a connection to Mother Earth. Environmentalists, farmers and gardeners wear it proudly in their aura. It gives a person the sense of belonging to the world and indicates that beliefs are firmly rooted in the ground. Skeletal ailments are associated with this colour.

Russet brown denotes a hard-working person with quiet assurance. It personifies 'industrious behaviour with restraint'.

Terracotta indicates a break with convention. Adolescents wishing to untie the so-called apron strings are drenched in it. Those who work within a bureaucratic system who dare to advance its thinking and policies are likely to have terracotta around their hands and legs.

Dark brown reflects common sense. It means that a person is practical, down to earth, systematic and self-disciplined. It reflects conventional behaviour.

GOLD

Gold is the colour of evolved consciousness. It is frequently depicted in halos around the heads of spiritual individuals such as Jesus Christ, Buddha, saints and other exceptionally holy people. I have seen it in the auras of charismatic spiritual leaders such as Father Bede Griffith and Sai Baba. Frequently, clairvoyants mistake golden yellow for gold because their eyes are not attuned to auric vibrations.

These two aura photographs show the colours of the author's aura when she is in different states of mind.

Pensive The combination of pale blue, indigo and magenta in the aura indicates that a person is relaxed, sensitive to their surroundings, open to opportunity and physically inspired in day-to-day life.

Healing The combination of magenta, orange and pink in the aura indicates a spiritual connection to the unconditional love of divine healing.

Photographs by
Aura Vision International

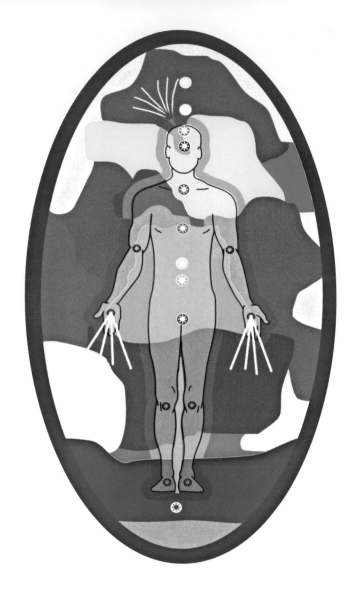

AURA ANALYSIS 1

Intuition is encouraging this person to sort the unnecessary issues from the necessary issues in his life, in order to create a new reality so that he can follow his vocation. Strength of character, together with an obsessive strength of self, make him egotistical. A need for greater effort is apparent in his aura, in order for new skills to be born and to bring ongoing traumas to rest. This will give his life a sense of balance. (Refer to *Colour in the Aura* for further information about the colours of this aura drawing.)

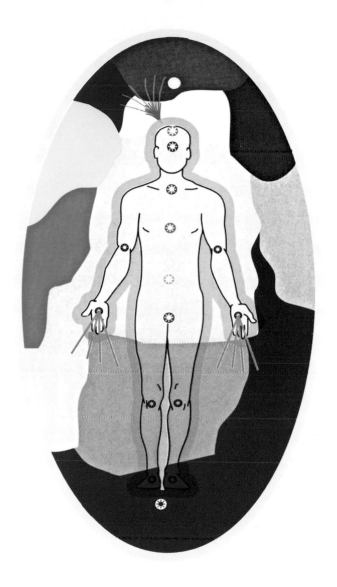

AURA ANALYSIS 2

This person is engaged in a loving relationship where passion is a dominant factor, and he is undergoing a physical change, as he becomes aware of emotional, intuitive and bodily sensations. Poor decision-making in the past has produced a lack of ambition. However, positive opportunities are apparent in his aura, which will serve to change his reality and enable him to overcome the frustration of the past traumas. A spirit, known to him in a past life, is expanding his sixth sense. (Refer to *Colour in the Aura* for further information about the colours in this aura drawing.)

COLOUR STIMULATION EXERCISE

Focus on the centre of the colour wheel. After a few seconds your eyes will see the coloured dots and your focus will quickly move around the wheel. The colour and size of the dots will change. Do this exercise for three to five minutes, twice a day, to expand the cones and rods in your eyes. This will enhance your auric colour viewing. To readjust your focus at the end of the exercise, gently close your eyes and allow any after images to fade completely.

GREEN

Pale green reflects spiritual advancement through the attunement to nature and the spirit realm. It is as calm and as tranquil as a sunny day in a rainforest. It is as refreshing as spring rain. It is as compassionate as a guardian angel. I have come to realise that those who have pale green in their aura are truly 'beautiful' people.

Lemon green (greenish yellow) is the shade of a liar and a cheat. Traces of this colour always indicate a deceitful streak in a person. If located in the outer layers of the aura it can mean that the person is locked into a deceitful reality caused by others. Often adolescents have an element of lemon green in their aura when peer group pressure is applied against their will.

Apple green is the healing force of new life. It causes new skills to be born at a subtle pace and is usually associated with health care professionals. When seen around the hands it denotes natural healing abilities. Near or around the feet it indicates that the person is on a healing journey.

Iridescent green indicates friendliness, reliability and open-mindedness. The average person carries a certain degree of this colour in their aura. If located around the thigh area, it can reflect an openness to the abundance of all the good things that life has to offer.

Emerald green when present in the aura indicates that an ongoing trauma is being put to rest in a subtle way. This colour has a healing effect on the emotions and causes a person to respond rather than react to a situation.

Emerald green-blue is the colour of the natural-born healer and depicts a rare quality. It is sometimes found in the auras of those employed in healing professions—spiritual healers, natural health practitioners, doctors, nurses, dentists, counsellors, charity workers and the like.

Jade represents a charitable nature and patterns of self-sacrifice with little or no expectation of anything in return. It is often found in the aura of those in religious orders.

Viridian (mid greenish-blue) indicates that the person is currently experiencing a period of emotional and mental stress which is depleting their vital and astral auras.

Olive green would have been seen in the aura of Charles Dickens's character Ebenezer Scrooge, for it reflects a miserly attitude and a person who does not trust easily. If this colour becomes muddy it indicates possessiveness.

Dark green reflects mental stress, either self-induced or externally influenced. If dark green is accompanied by the colour yellow, then the mind is locked into a self-doubting, self-denial and self-critical phase.

Green-silver grey only appears in an aura when a person is locked into negative memories of their experience while in the womb. Its misty appearance tends to cloud the aura.

Turquoise is the colour of positive and obsessive growth. People who are focused on developing their character and skills, to rise above their birth-class, often have turquoise in their aura over a period of years.

GREY

Pale grey indicates that the person is a victim of poor decision-making. Those who feel trapped by their decisions, such as their selection of a career path or relationship, usually have pale grey located around the hip and knee areas of the aura.

Silver grey shows a leaning towards feminine expression. Traces of this colour are commonly located in the aura of creative individuals and those who work in health care professions. A person practising yoga, martial arts, meditation and other forms of spiritual enlightenment will also have traces of silver grey in their aura.

Charcoal grey denotes depression and suffocation of energy. When teamed with pink the matter becomes serious because of its connection with suicidal tendencies.

ORANGE

Apricot is the colour of caring communication. It is usually seen in the auras of doting parents, counsellors and negotiators. It is my favourite auric colour because it shows that a person is benevolent and supportive of other human beings. I see it frequently in the auras of the members of the Salvation Army and Hare Krishna disciples.

Orange is the colour of motivation, communication and socialisation and is commonly seen in the aura of successful people, especially entrepreneurs. Politicians during election campaigns are saturated in orange auric vibrations. Bubbly, outgoing personalities are also immersed in it. Orange represents vitality at its best, the personality known as a 'live wire'. Those who have orange in their aura permanently are born to rule. Their sense of responsibility is usually devoid of the lust for personal power. They are excellent mixers, able to communicate with any class of person, rich or poor. When orange appears around the hands it shows that the person is well organised, and working to better the community.

Pumpkin (golden orange) indicates both firm goals and a methodology by which to achieve them. It also indicates self-control. This colour can frequently be seen in the aura of students undertaking study and exams which create or enhance career opportunities.

Orange-brown denotes a lack of ambition, laziness and a careless attitude. Too much of this colour in the aura may also indicate kidney trouble.

Orange-red shows indecisiveness and a weak will. It usually appears in the aura near the feet, signalling that the person is easily led by others.

PINK

Pale pink in small doses signifies love. In abundance, it can indicate immaturity or a modest or withdrawn individual. Abused children usually have the colour pink strewn across the chest area of the aura.

Pink madder represents loyalty, commitment and obsessiveness. Most newlyweds have it in their aura, as do individuals belonging to religious sects.

Salmon pink represents vocation. Those following their true vocation in life may find this colour almost permanently in their aura.

Iridescent pink represents lust at its height of animalistic passion. Some adolescent males as they stroll along in search of a sexual conquest are aurically ablaze in iridescent pink.

Dusty pink reflects immaturity. Often when a person is fooling around this colour will temporarily enter his or her aura. However, it becomes a serious matter when it appears in the aura regularly, as it shows a lack of responsibility and in some cases, emotional and mental disorders.

PURPLE

Lavender is the colour of developing psychic abilities. It usually means that the person has experienced an incident which has spiritually uplifted or awakened them. Hence they feel the flow of an inner 'knowing' and the sense of being connected to a higher purpose. Any person who has had a near death experience has the colour lavender in one or many areas of their aura.

Lilac is the colour of spiritual balance. The harmony it projects into the aura causes a person to feel at peace. It is commonly seen in the auras of the elderly. I believe this is because they have lived their life, fought most of their battles and generally reached a certain level of acceptance. In addition, the prospect of death is frequently in their reality. Those who practise their religious beliefs bring into their aura pale green, which when blended with the lilac represents that they are charitable, caring, gracious human beings.

Magenta represents change linked to synchronicity. In short, it means the individual will be in the right place, at the right time, for the right opportunity for their personal advancement. In the aura of entrepreneurs, magenta is often located around the head, feet and hands.

Mauve is the colour of humility. Unfortunately, few people in western society today have this colour in their aura. Many members of religious orders attract this colour into their aura through their ritualist practice of self-sacrifice, sharing and caring.

Imperial purple is perhaps the most common colour found in the aura of those seeking a 'new age' path. The colour reflects stimulation of the intuition, awakening a person to the depth of their inner self, and is usually around the head as a result of increased dream activity. Those with purple in their aura are inclined to be overbearing with their spiritual ideas and philosophy.

Grape reflects a need for a greater effort on the part of the individual. Children and university students who don't study enough often have this colour clouding their aura.

Violet is the colour of the soul's vocation. It represents unlimited spiritual wisdom and is achieved by an alignment of the mind, emotions, body and spirit. Genuine gurus have violet in their aura when preaching to the masses. Those with violet in their aura exhibit humility.

Blue violet is not commonly seen in an aura. It is a sign of transcendent idealism.

Red violet denotes the soul's creative inspiration for the expansion of personal power.

RED

Carmine reflects unexpected changes and transmutation. It usually appears in an aura when the person is subconsciously seeking change.

Vermilion indicates creativity and strong emotions. Whenever you meet a dynamic, creative or charismatic person, this colour is probably woven throughout their aura. Whenever you do anything with great passion, you can be assured that vermilion is in your aura. When you lose your temper, get impatient or argue, vermilion stripes appear in your aura.

Rustic red reflects impulsiveness, nervousness and aggression. Anyone who has a short temper has a degree of rustic red in their aura.

Scarlet red reflects an overdose of ego. It also signifies lust and an overpowering passion. When this colour is the dominating colour in the aura an individual may fantasise frequently.

Crimson is the colour that reinforces natural creative skills. In addition, it expands a person's clarity of vision, allowing them to attune more deeply to creativity. However, an over-abundance of this colour shows that the person is obsessive and possessive.

Maroon is the colour of self-empowerment and firm direction. A person changing their lifestyle or career will have this colour around his or her feet. It also signals that the person is drawing on nervous energy in their physical body.

Claret strengthens your determination and secures your focus on your vocation. This colour is often seen in the aura of someone who is changing a career path or overcoming a trau-matic encounter. When combined with pale blue, it shows a person who is outwardly strong but inwardly weak. An abun-dance of claret in the aura is inclined to make a person quick-tempered, quick to act, domineering and overbearing.

SILVER

Silver (metallic) is the colour of the link between creation and the spirit realm. Mediums, and healers who regularly converse with the spirit realm, are cocooned in plaited silver and violet. During ovulation, most women display minute silver and orange star-like vibrations throughout their aura, indicating fertility and new life. I believe that the male species has been able to subconsciously detect these indicators, and that this auric code has ensured the growth and survival of the human race. This energy is also present in the mother's aura throughout pregnancy.

Zinc (silvery grey colour) is often seen around the sexual organs of either males or females when parenthood is pending.

WHITE

Cream is the colour of putting your best foot forward. When it appears in the aura, the earthly and spiritual vibrations are aligning for personal advancement. I get very excited when I see it for it means that you can't put a foot wrong. Consequently, I advise my clients to reach for the sky.

Pearl reflects the purification of mind, body and soul. Those who are devoted to the advancement of spiritual enlightenment, as well as outstanding mediums and healers who converse with spirits, have small amounts of pearl in their aura from time to time. I suspect that Christ and Buddha, to name but two, would have had a pure pearl aura, for this is the perfect aura. For most people, the colour pearl appears in the aura moments before death. I believe this is to cleanse and balance the self in preparation for the transition from the physical realm to the spirit realm.

Transparent white indicates the presence of telepathic abilities. This is easily evaluated by the number of times an individual knows in advance who is going to visit them or telephone them. Transparent white also has a divine lineage.

White wash indicates that an individual is about to move through a physical change which will affect their lifestyle, finances, relationships, health or occupation. The change is usually disruptive but, in the long term, will have a very positive outcome. In other words 'a change for the better'. Little white lies, commonly referred to in day-to-day life, manifest themselves as white wash energy in the aura.

YELLOW

Pale yellow indicates a poor state of mind or a timid character. Individuals who have been intimidated by others show the emotional scars by the presence of this colour in their aura.

Primrose yellow reflects optimism and new learning. Those beginning a new career have primrose yellow around the head area. Young children, on their first day of school, exhibit this colour in their aura.

Lemon yellow shows that the mind of the individual has strength of direction and is currently sorting and sifting the necessary from the unnecessary issues in their life.

Buttercup yellow indicates that the mind is strictly focused on a major issue or course of action.

Golden yellow reflects the elevation of the mind to a higher sense of consciousness. It indicates great inspiration and in some cases revitalisation of the mind.

Mustard indicates manipulative mind games. It shows a deceitful nature because of how an individual can be a friend and foe at the same time.

Orange yellow denotes excessive thinking and a dogmatic personality. This person has a need to be recognised for even the smallest contribution or will consequently feel deprived and become analytical and over-critical. The person may suffer from constant headaches.

Straw yellow indicates people who dream the idle hours away in useless and purposeless visions and reveries. Their impractical nature usually also creates financial stress which is seen in the aura as a plait consisting of various shades of grey and straw yellow.

Colour combinations in the aura

Although you have just learnt what the different auric colours mean, when certain colours are in close proximity they produce a new meaning through the combination of their energies.

When I was seven years old my grandmother died. Prior to her death, colours of lemon yellow, maroon, magenta and silver splashed across her feet, while grey and black sat like a hard, impenetrable blob to one side of her head. At the time, I had a rudimentary understanding of what the colours individually meant. But, it took her death to awaken my consciousness to the meaning of colour combinations in the aura. She died of a cerebral haemorrhage. An aunt found her lying on her bedroom floor in an unconscious state, a condition that lasted for days before she passed over. Unfortunately, children weren't permitted to visit her in hospital so I didn't see the colours of impending death until several years later.

The variation in colour combinations in the aura is almost limitless and it is impossible for me to describe each one in this book. Many combinations are specifically associated with a particular illness or situation in life, so I have selected a number of common combinations which I am able to describe in a fairly general way. It is only with experience that you will be able to accurately read the more complicated and unusual combinations.

Mourning

Lemon yellow, varying shades of grey with a combined cloak of pale pink and blue indicate that a person is in mourning.

I remember clearly my mother as she came through the doorway and told me that my grandmother had died. In later years my mother exclaimed how surprised she was, that when given the news, I simply smiled at her and returned to my play. She said I never asked any questions or discussed it until I reached adulthood. The colours of my grandmother's aura had faded rapidly and the vital aura had lost its vibrance, so I knew that she would die soon. Therefore I wasn't shocked when I was told that she had died.

I recall at that time my mother's aura was locked into the pattern of mourning.

Personal transition

Autumn tones throughout the aura indicate a settling period
for the individual. Some may feel they are 'stuck' because
of the temporary reflection period and lack of activity in
their life. The aura may look lifeless, but it is only a phase of
transition.

Terminal illness

Charcoal grey, muddy brown and pale pink indicate that a
person is terminally ill. When I was thirteen years old, the
shades of death became known to me. My girlfriend Sandra's
mother was seriously ill. A hole in her heart rendered her low
on energy and personal strength. Consequently, Sandra had
to do all the housework and manage the household accounts,
as her father was frequently away from home with his work.
Apparently he needed to do this because of the enormous
medical bills they encountered weekly.

Sandra's mother's aura intrigued me because it rarely
altered. It never shone brightly or sparkled in the sunlight.
The sprays of lucid colours found in a healthy aura never
brought hers to life. Instead, the drabness of fading colour
was always present. She had become very miserable because
her life was sheer misery. This produced shades of grey and
muddy brown in her aura with interwoven pink ribbon-like
threads, giving the appearance of stitching the misery in place.
One day when visiting Sandra, I noticed a splash of orange
piercing through her mother's hazy aura when she attempted
to hang some washing on the line. The motivational strength
of orange encouraged her participation in life. However, this
minimal exertion had her in hospital one day later. In the few
years that Sandra and I were friends, her mother spoke no
more than five hundred words to me. She always managed a
smile and faint hello. Little did she know that she was one of
my greatest teachers.

Death and the after life

As I became more and more familiar with the human aura I saw that there are many causes of death, apart from illness, for example, loneliness, poor self-esteem, self-sacrifice and anger. However, impending death is generally represented in the aura by the combination of magenta, silver and gold.

It was when Sandra and I caught the train to visit her mother in hospital that I first saw the step-by-step process of death in the human aura. Directly in line with her knees was a black and grey streaked blob of energy. Over the heart remained pale lemon, blue and black as it had always been, and is quite common with ailments of the heart. A folded layer of magenta, grey and black enshrined the aura as if embalming it, the soft pale grey clinging to the magenta with its power to connect to the spirit realm. The sprays of magenta spread through every layer of the aura to its outer realm. The blue mist of the etheric aura displayed sprinkles of mystical silver and divine gold, increasing in number by the hour as the blackness engulfed her physical body. It was then I realised how the etheric layer of the aura carries the soul through the physical restrictions to a reality of altered consciousness that we know as death.

Restricted self-expression

When dusty pink and grey are combined in the aura, this generally indicates that a person has restricted or buried their self-expression tendencies.

While I was drawing the aura of a young woman in her early twenties, I quickly pointed out to her that her relationship was killing her. Spontaneously, she told me about all the allergies and illnesses she had experienced in the past two years. The creativeness of red in her aura was entwined with the vulnerability of pink and the self-destruction of grey. The dusty pink of commitment and vocation was also clouded in grey. However, claret with its vigour of the phoenix rising from the ashes was hovering in the outskirts of the aura, waiting for an opportunity to show its worth. I knew that if she made the necessary changes in her life, she would be well once again, and I made a few suggestions.

A year later, she came to see me at a festival, and I could not believe my eyes. A radiant, highly energetic person stood before me. She told me how she, herself, had seen the need for major change in her life, how illness was now a thing of the past, and how happy she had become.

Thwarted love

Thwarted love can be seen in the aura as a combination of yellow, green, pale blue and charcoal grey.

So often the emotional heart chains itself to a whipping post and life serves us a daily meal of punishment. Often we are too weak to stand or find the courage to walk away.

A middle-aged man, married to a women who had betrayed him for the past thirteen years, requested that I sketch his aura. At a quick glance I could see that she had just left him. Looking him straight in the eyes I said, 'I think you know how bedraggled your aura is.' He shrugged his shoulders and said, 'I want to see how miserable I feel.' I told him that he was throwing his money away. He retorted defensively, so I proceeded. His aura was drenched with the self-deceit of yellowy green, interlaced with the sensitivity of pale blue and hopelessness of charcoal grey. Pockets of dusty pink and apricot showed his commitment to his wife and his children. My heart cried out to him when I could not locate any colours of change or advancement. All I could predict was a long path of hopelessness. So I advised that he have counselling.

Loneliness

Loneliness is depicted in the aura by a combination of pink and mustard. Regularly a man in his mid-twenties visits my exhibit at major new age festivals in New South Wales, Australia. The fluctuating patterns in his aura indicate poor self-esteem. Since childhood he has suffered with a life-threatening illness which has stunted his growth, and consequently his physique is that of a fourteen-year-old boy. The vulnerability of pink, and mustard energy with its manipulative, determination of mind, have smothered the layers of his aura, ensuring his focus would remain fixed on his loneliness. In order to rise above this restrictive pattern he would need to expand his self-esteem.

Mental stress

As people in western society lead more and more hectic and stressful lives, bottle green and muddy brown take hold in the human aura. Together these colours indicate chronic mental stress due to being trapped in a rut.

As an exercise one day while I was sitting in a train, I devised a game to avoid boredom on a long and tiring journey. 'Spot the stress' I called it. To my amazement, only two people in the carriage were completely free of the colours. Some of my fellow travellers were bogged down in jobs they didn't like, others were trapped in poor relationships, while the remainder were in debt. This experience awakened me to the stress that human beings carry when they are not free to be their individual selves.

Suicide

Mesh-like patterns of muddy brown, medium grey, pink and bottle green woven in a screen over the vibrance of the vital layer of the aura, inhibit a person's sense of connectiveness to the world. This is the path of suicide.

A nineteen-year-old man approached me to draw his aura. At a glance I could see that the path that he was treading was choking his very life-force. I noticed an older woman of similar resemblance, hovering in the background, and I asked him if she was his mother. When he answered yes, I breathed a sigh of relief, and suggested that she would be interested in the revelations of his aura, so he went outside and invited her to join us.

Looking at his mother, I addressed my enquiry of her son's withdrawn behaviour to her. She immediately expressed the family's concern. He had been eating meals by himself and generally ignoring all family activity. Interaction with his friends had also dropped off. She further explained that she and her husband suspected that he was on drugs. I promptly quashed this allegation.

The three of us determined what had led to his emotional weakness: unemployment since leaving school, a break up with his girlfriend, a lack of money to entertain himself, jealousy of a successful younger brother, and his skinny physique. With counselling he overcame his ordeal and today is happy and content.

Bankruptcy

Whenever I come across the aura of a bankrupt I think of the lepers of biblical times and how they were cast out of society. For this is what their aura says to the world. Matted shades of grey, pink, muddy brown, bottle green, black and mustard yellow twist and turn throughout the aura, like an ivy vine choking a tree as it grows.

A middle-aged woman waited patiently in a queue to se me for an aura drawing. When she stepped forward, I looked over her aura, placed my hand on my colour pencils and paused for a split second, unsure about how the woman would react. Obviously my body language said it all because she lent forward, placed her hand on mine and said, 'It's all right Judith, I know the worst of it.' From her head to her knees her aura displayed the colours of bankruptcy. When I explained what I could see, the woman told me of the death of her husband and of the debts of the business he had left behind. He had died suddenly and not left her well provided for. Six months after his death, her only son was severely hurt in a motorcycle accident and died three weeks later. So, in the course of seven months, she had lost her husband and son, her house and her source of income. At fifty-two years of age, she had to find a new beginning.

Due to the sadness of this tale, I searched her aura deeply and thoroughly and found the richness of claret forcing its way to the surface. I was then able to paint a positive future for her. I knew it would cause her to rise above the trauma, with the strength and determination to be reborn.

Deception

The combination of mustard and olive green implies that the person has a deceptive nature.

One of the most embarrassing situations in which my aura readings have placed me was at a time when I was rushed off my feet at a major festival. A lovely young woman had her aura drawn and all appeared to be straightforward. She was madly in love and so her aura was glowing. Her boyfriend, some years older than herself, was next in line. I looked at his aura and almost took three steps back. I drew it quickly, and invited him to step to the back of my stall for privacy. A pattern of mustard and olive green was woven like a tartan cloth about the knee area. I quizzed him about business deals, work, financial loans, as I searched for a clue for the deception these colours represented. The girlfriend stepped forward, excused herself and suggested that she wait nearby. Seconds after she moved away, he told me of his wife and children at home and of his affair with this young woman. Well, I didn't know where to look. The poor man thought it would be fun having his aura drawn. Instead, it drove a wedge into the reality of the deception that he was creating for the people in his life.

The inventor

The creativeness of red, the mind power of lemon yellow and the creative inspiration of crimson, when situated in the hands depict creative and inventive skills.

While working in Western Australia, an eager wife ushered her reluctant husband towards me to have his aura drawn. A tall, stately chap, dressed in beach attire, he looked at me as if I were a freak. I returned his glare and said, 'Tell me what you have invented.' A confirming chuckle came from his family who were looking on. In orderly stripes across his hands, the aura revealed an intensity of red, lemon yellow and crimson. He was so astounded that he decided to pay attention to everything I had to say. A more intense reading showed that marketing the product would be slow, but in the long term very successful. I noticed as he walked away that a lightness was in his step.

The entrepreneur

The motivational power of orange combined with the creativity of red indicates a successful entrepreneurial path.

A married couple in their mid-thirties approached me for an aura analysis. I threw my hands up in the air with excitement, exclaiming, 'Let me be the first to congratulate you.'

They smiled and waited for a further explanation. Both auras showed they had recently sold everything to raise capital to launch a new business venture. As they excitedly kissed me on both cheeks, the husband explained how they were simply following their gut instincts. I was the lucky person to be able to tell them that their decision would pay dividends.

The self-starter

An aura predominantly draped in doe-skin, orange and apple green indicates that the person will continually move forward in everything they choose to do.

During a consultation with the family doctor, she talked to me of my mother's health, and I became enthralled with her aura. Her mind processed demands in an orderly, systematic manner allowing her to effectively follow her chosen path. A doctor with a very busy practice, she definitely showed none of the tell-tale signs of a hectic lifestyle.

The mother-to-be

A woman stood nervously waiting for her aura to be drawn and I noticed that the swirling colour around and across the pelvic area was pulsating the spiritual balance of lilac and the unconditional love of pink. While drawing her aura, my intuition told me to scan her body in the same way I do to diagnose an illness. I concentrated on the pastel glow. Sure enough, it was a developing foetus. When I announced my findings, the woman cried and then asked me to check again. She told me of her fourteen-year-long struggle to have a child and of her medical encounters. Embarrassed by so many false alarms, she hadn't gone to the doctor for verification of her pregnancy. After she had missed two menstrual periods, I could not help but pick up on the embryo in the womb. So eager was this mother-to-be to share the news with her husband that she rushed away from the stall in pursuit of a telephone, leaving her handbag behind. When she returned to collect it, I noticed that her aura had come alive with new life. I can remember thinking how pleased I was to play a role in such joy.

Master of martial arts

At first I thought that I was seeing things. I had never seen anything like it before. Yellow and silver light streamed from the man's hands and feet. I scanned his aura looking for additional clues so I could understand what I was seeing. A halo of golden yellow light formed a glowing cocoon around the aura. The spiritual awareness of silver and yellow with its power of the mind made me realise that the man was a martial arts expert. On questioning him he revealed himself as an aikido master. I remember being in awe of his inner power.

Since that time, I have come to notice that these colour combinations are common among devotees of martial arts, but I have never seen colours as intense as his.

The healer

I once met a man who felt that he'd been a failure all his life. His sunken chin and protruding cheek bones made him look more like a clay model than a human being. His opinion of himself had been formed by a trail of failed attempts at establishing a career path. However, what I saw was quite the opposite. Gentle sprays of apricot and apple green energy told me of his caring nature and talent for comforting people in their hour of need. So, when he asked for advice and direction, I told him of his natural healing skills. At first his poor self-image made him refuse to hear what I was saying. However, a friend reinforced my words by relating an incident in which he had intervened and been a tremendous help. Years later we met again. He was surrounded by an enthusiastic audience delivering a lecture on healing. It was obvious that he had found his life's path.

Born psychic

I have lost count of the number of people who ask me to confirm their psychic gifts. The vast majority are wishful thinkers, but genuine psychics show violet and silver rays around the head area.

I remember meeting a group of young female university students. Among them was a shy girl, standing in the shadows of the others as they jostled for position to be first to see me. I stood up and pointed to the small, inconspicuous girl. She came forward and I talked to her of her imaginary childhood friends and of her continuous lucid dreams, as well as her ability to predict future events. Her friends were unwilling to believe that she had such rich insight. As I drew her aura, their eyes were fixed on the violet and silver rays which indicate the highest level of spiritual awareness and interaction with the spirit realm. I advised her to seek guidance from a spiritualist church so that her gift would not be tainted or misused by the trendy sects of the 'new age' movement, but be allowed to develop and expand naturally for the greater service of humanity.

The motivator

The intertwined energy strands of motivational orange, the sensitivity of pale blue and crimson's clarity of creative vision indicate a motivated person.

A young, vibrant, but lost seventeen-year-old came to see me. It's hard to determine how to plan your life's path at such a young age, so he thought that I could help. His marks at school had been below average, leaving him in a bit of a quandary as to how to apply his limited skills. I listened to him plead his case to me as I sketched his aura. He paused for a moment to question the curious grin on my face. The motivational colours were draped over his shoulders to his knees, letting me know that this young man could be successful in the advertising field.

The spiritual vocation

A person connected to a spiritual vocation will have salmon pink and pink madder filtering softly through the pale blue and violet clouds of their aura. Silver sprays of auric light will be seen shining upwards about the head.

A woman dressed in plain, drab street clothes, which did nothing to enhance her lifeless skin, smiled serenely while approaching me to draw her aura. 'Do I call you Sister?' I dared to ask. The astonished look and gentle nod of her head confirmed that she was a nun. The mixture of these colours reminded me of the time I had lived away from home as a teenager, when I often saw nuns helping and feeding the poor and the homeless.

A holy sacrament

The silver auric light which shines out of the soul chakra and surrounds the head, dappled with violet, can frequently be seen in the aura of a Christian who, as a child, received the sacrament of confirmation, and continued their spiritual search, whether through religion or metaphysics.

Adults can be shocked to see these colours in their aura, especially when they have turned their back on family religion. All I can say is that this powerful ritual makes a significant contribution to connecting the mind, body and soul.

Placement of colours in the aura

Although colour in an aura resembles the flow of colourful clouds melting into one another, an understanding of the position of individual colours and combinations of colour within the layers of the aura is vitally important to your overall understanding of what an aura tells you. Colours move about the aura rapidly taking up their position to represent personal character and the destiny of an individual, as you will see in the following descriptions.

Back of the head (casual chakra and spirit attachment)

If colourful rays emanate from this area, this indicates the connection of a spirit guide and the nature of its guidance. The colour changes only at the direction of the spirit guide. Royal blue indicates the attachment of a deceased relative, whereas dark green indicates a spirit that has known you in a past life.

While working at a festival a group of middle-aged women approached me to draw their auras and by all accounts they were pleased with the results. When I focused on the last member of the group I noticed that the outer layers of her aura kept changing. Attuning my eyes to the higher mental aura, I saw one deceased relative appear, then another, then another. Three in all had made their debut. When I declared my findings, the woman burst into tears and told me of the death of her sister and two nieces in a recent car accident. I was able to assure her that they had appeared so she would know that they were happy.

Head

Colours surrounding the head indicate the focus of the mind, its inspiration, reactive behaviour, and general thinking processes. A cloud of red to either side of the head suggests that the person has recently been angered by someone or something whereas a yellow cloud indicates that the person has been thinking hard.

There is rarely only one colour around the head due to the mind's range and frequency of thinking impulses. Colour in this area changes rapidly, sometimes every five minutes when the mind is very active, or it can be as slow as every half hour, depending on what a person is focused on. When a person is focused on writing a book, composing music or carrying out intense research, the mind may hold the same colours around the head for weeks on end as the person continually thinks about the same thing.

While working at a major festival, I suggested to a man that he come back and see me in half an hour's time when his aura had calmed down. It was obvious that he had rushed to the festival straight from work and on the way had been upset by another person. When he had relaxed himself, I was able to read his mind's focus and provide him with some worthwhile advice and direction.

Shoulders

If a person is feeling burdened by life, a caramel colour formation shows across the shoulders, thereby reflecting their mind's focus and what they are carrying forward into the future. The same situation occurs when a person is excited by a new direction in their lives, but in this case the colour is red. The colour usually remains fixed in this position for up to two weeks.

Arms

Servants of the mind, your arms display how you are currently conducting your life in line with the focus of your mind, and how you interact with your instinctive self as well as relatives, friends and the world. Claret around the arms indicates a person working towards overpowering adversity. Whereas pale pink indicates that the person is in a loving relationship. Here the colour changes on average every one to six weeks.

Hands

Not only do the hands indicate how you express yourself, they can also reflect your skills and talents. When the arms are coloured orange and the hands are coloured red, I know that the person has entrepreneurial skills and can succeed at anything they creatively choose to do.

While working in Brisbane, Australia, I had the pleasure of confirming a very gifted young girl's career choice in the acting profession. Her hands were coloured pale blue and red.

I was puzzled by the hands of a man in his late fifties because they indicated to me that he had healing skills, whereas other parts of his aura referred to his mundane labouring work. He explained to me that he had been a medical practitioner in Spain but that his medical qualifications were not recognised in Australia.

Colours which relate to personal expression can change every one to four weeks, whereas colours indicating skills and talents can remain for years.

Under the arms

This is the first place that I look when I do an aura reading. The area under the arms indicates the behaviour of your directional path. It is the culmination of thought and proposed action. Colours in this area normally relate to the emotions, such as pale blue or pink, or are motivational such as orange or tones of red. Colours in this area generally change every three weeks to four months.

A woman who had left her abusive husband appeared physically frail and fearful of the future. However, when I saw the colour claret under her arms, I knew that she was preparing to rise like the phoenix from the ashes with the greatest strength and determination.

Hip line

The force of your direction in life and connection to reality is indicated by the colours that flow around the contour of the hip line. The same woman that I described in the under arms section had buttercup yellow in this position, which indicated that nothing was going to change her mind—she definitely desired change. Whereas, if I had seen charcoal grey I would have known that she felt she had no way out.

As the auric force acts in accordance with each feeling, thought and action, the colour in this area will alter slowly, changing every one to six months.

Legs

How, and at what pace, we travel towards our goals and destiny is indicated by the colour around the leg area. The colours can show if you are unable to reach your life's goal (raw sienna), if the pace of change will slow down in the next few months (royal blue), or if you will succeed as mentally or emotionally planned, which can be indicated by carmine, amber, dusty pink and grape.

The colours of destiny usually remain in this area for several months.

Feet

This is the second place I look when doing an aura reading because it tells me if the person has been locked into a negative or positive holding pattern for the last six months, and if the pattern will change within the next six months. Therefore, colours around the feet area generally remain fixed for four to six months.

Bottle green tells me that the person's progress is blocked by mental stress, while magenta tells that the person will benefit from an opportunity.

Colour blocks

Many of us have 'colour-blockages' which inhibit our interpretation of the true vibration and essence of both colour and the aura. Most blocks relate to past emotional encounters. As a child you may have been frightened by a stranger at a bus stop which had a dark green seat and a yellow and black signpost. These colours then become associated with fear in your subconscious mind. Consequently, when you observe your blocked colour in an aura, you may experience a sense of caution, fear, withdrawal or rage.

The only colour that I disliked for years was aqua. When I saw it in a person's aura, it gave rise to feelings of frustration and imprisonment. It was not, however, until I underwent some self-counselling in order to overcome the pain that I had caused my parents during my adolescence, that I recalled the colour of the doors at the back of the house. When feeling miserable and trapped, I would sit and sulk in our courtyard. Four pale aqua doors faced the yard. Hence, I developed a colour block from that short, but turbulent, period in my life—the doors being my sign for adolescent imprisonment.

Recognising colour blocks

Self-reflection has encouraged me to respond to people who

say they hate a particular colour. It's not that a particular colour offends us, it's the associated unconscious memory it represents that does.

A dear friend of mine was blocked by the colour orange. On deep reflection, she realised that her mother's kitchen, although multi-coloured, was dominated by this colour. Trauma and frustration was all that her mother had known, causing her to take her own life.

So, my friend had unconsciously grown up associating the colour orange with her mother's suicide. Once she realised this, the colour orange was immediately released from the trauma.

A mother sought my advice for her eight-year-old child's behavioural problems. He had become aggressive and violent. I had the mother describe his family background and then the colour of his bedroom and toys. Quickly, I assessed that the colour red was the trigger of his emotional outbursts. The mother explained how the child, at age four, had awoken from an afternoon nap to find his mother in a pool of blood, caused by the cutting of her wrists. An adoptive family was found and he responded very well to them and to counselling, but suddenly his behaviour had reverted. I suggested that his bedroom be painted pale green and that all red items be removed. With these minor changes, his adoptive mother reported that her son's behaviour had improved almost overnight.

It's quite amazing how we build up a resentment or dislike for a colour because of our life experiences. Being aware of them not only helps you to interpret auras more accurately, but can also help you to emotionally evolve. Remember that colour blindness in one or more colours does not inhibit a person's ability to see and read the human aura and is no way considered to be a colour block. This visual handicap can easily be overcome by using your perception to interpret an aura.

Exercise

Explore your range of colourful thoughts and expressions by filling in the gaps of this story, using the colours that automatically spring to mind as you read through it.

I walked along a_____brick path through a dense_____forest. The air was fresh and crisp. The sun produced a dappled light as it filtered through the_____canopy of the trees. A_____statue stood at the crossroad of the path. Its inscription said 'The_____light is ahead for all those who seek healing. To the left is the_____light for those who seek self-forgiveness. To the right is the_____light for those who seek courage. To the rear is what has passed.' As I stood pondering which road to take, a large_____eagle flew overhead. I looked up at the_____sky with its fluffy_____clouds and suddenly felt free. The ease of my journey took on a_____calm. I could feel my soul cry out with joy as I transcended. A_____mist moved towards me. Within seconds I felt its love. My mind was at ease. My heart beat calm and secure. I could feel the expansion of my intuitiveness. Colours of_____, _____and_____filled my mind's eye. The rhythm of life flowed through my veins unburdening all that was me. A_____ray gently pierced my body to connect with my soul. In grace I was reborn as a_____being.

Determining your colour blocks

Use the exercise that follows to determine if you are blocked by one or more colours.

Exercise

- Tick the colours you like least and note why.
- Think of traumatic experiences in your life to ascertain the colour link and nature of the blockage.
- Proceed with the 'Releasing colour blocks' exercise (page 127).

[ ] Apricot _____

[ ] Aqua _____

[ ] Black _____

[ ] Blue _____

[ ] Brown _____

[ ] Cream _____

[ ] Green _____

[ ] Grey _____

[ ] Maroon _____

[ ] Orange _____

[ ] Pink _____

[ ] Purple _____

[ ] Red _____

[ ] Silver _____

[ ] White _____

[ ] Yellow _____

The following two exercises can also help to highlight colour blocks and are designed specifically to stimulate colour perception. However, as described below, to release a deep-seated colour block you need to revisit the memory which caused it.

Exercises

PERCEIVING COLOUR VIBRATIONS

1. Place six different coloured squares of paper or non-patterned fabric in individual envelopes. Shuffle the envelopes and place them on a table in front of you.
2. Sit, relaxed, breathing deeply and gently. Allow the mind to reach a state of floating peace. This usually takes about five to ten minutes.
3. Keep your eyes closed and pick up an envelope and sit, quietly and still, with it rested between the palms of your hands. Feel the electromagnetic force of the hands penetrate the envelope.
4. Allow a colour to float into your mind. Hold it for a few moments so that your intuition can inform you whether this is the colour in the envelope.
5. When you have intuitively arrived at the colour, open the envelope and check it for accuracy. Put the envelope aside regardless of the outcome.
6. Repeat steps 1–5 until you have worked through three of the envelopes, so that you don't exhaust the intuitive mind.
7. Take a ten-minute break, then repeat the exercise using the remaining three envelopes.
8. Repeat this exercise as often as you can to stimulate your intuitive perception of colour vibrations.

CONNECTING WITH COLOUR VIBRATIONS

I encourage my students to do this exercise as often as possible. Not only does it stimulate the senses, it also encourages you to explore your own interpretation of colour and colour emanations. Although it has no time framework, twenty minutes to half an hour will recharge your batteries, leaving you with a sense of renewal.

1. Sit opposite a person with whom you feel comfortable.

2. Connect with each other by the palms of the hands. They should lie flat, one person's hands on top of the other's.
3. Relax, close your eyes, and tune into your feelings.
4. Feel the rhythmic pace of the breath as you relax into each other's energy patterns.
5. Explore your senses for three major colours. Let them drift into your mind slowly and gently.
6. Gauge the shades of the colours. Are they dark, medium or light? What do you feel about these colours? Let your feelings explore your emotional and perceptive responses.
7. Allow yourself to fall into the magnetic 'floating' of this exercise to gain its full benefit.

Releasing colour blocks

Once you have determined your colour blockages, you need to address the associated trauma to ensure your smooth flow of auric vision and perception. The following exercise will help you to do this.

Exercise

1. Sit in a comfortable chair in a quiet location where you will not be disturbed.
2. Breathe slowly and deeply, allowing every muscle in the body to totally relax.
3. When you feel that the tension of the physical body has dissipated, allow your mind to recapture the memory of the trauma associated with the colour.
4. Imagine the colour embracing the memory, caressing and soothing it.
5. Feel the release of trauma, as the memory grows stronger and becomes comfortable.

You can master this exercise by practising it regularly for twenty minutes each day.

I advise all my students to go to an art store and purchase a full complement of colour pencils or crayons (seventy or more) to familiarise themselves with the various colours and to develop a working knowledge of them. Attunement to, and knowledge of, colour is important for accuracy in aura readings. I cannot stress this enough. Everyone needs to determine any colour blockages and their origins and then to release them.

5

HEALTH AND THE AURA

He who desires but acts not breeds pestilence.
A dead body revenges not injuries.

William Blake

When I look at an aura I can see its life-force rhythmically beating in colourful vibrance. The pulses of the breath and the blood fall into tune with what appears to me as the essence of life. The aura is crystal clear with a healthy range of colours all indicating the reality and aspirations of the individual. Well, this is the mirror image all of us should enjoy when we are healthy.

Stress from the pace of modern day city living can be seen in the aura as a dim version of the naturally vibrant self. During the peak hour rush busy city streets are flushed with auras scrambling to expand and contract in order to renew and restore themselves and refresh the total self. The auras of people clambering onto buses and trains merge, and within moments individuals pick up the stresses of their fellow travellers. Should they then return to a home filled with tension, the aura is unable to revitalise itself.

Unless city workers free themselves of stress through

relaxation or meditative exercises, the self grows dimmer and dimmer, making the person ill-at-ease. Notice the first part of this word is ill, this is because stress and fatigue can make you very sick. Often, during a stressful period, hereditary physical weakness is exacerbated and may even extend to new areas of the body and cause disease.

Ill health is depicted in the aura by a number of patterns and colours which may appear suddenly when a person is under attack from a virus or bacteria, or manifest themselves slowly over years as a result of unresolved emotional and physical issues. Chakras relating to specific areas of the body may be clogged, inhibiting the flow of the body's vital energy.

In healing sessions, once I have noted the patterns of the aura in my mind, I scan the person's physical body with my hands, using what is called 'extra-sensory touch'. My hands intuitively connect the auric patterns to the physical ailments and produce a diagnosis, and I can then suggest the appropriate treatment for my client. I enjoy an ever-increasing number of referrals from orthodox medical practitioners asking if I can detect and define the evasive or mysterious disorders suffered by their patients.

My worldwide healing work has exposed me to people from all walks of life, with a variety of temporary and terminal illnesses, thus allowing me to determine the auric patterns associated with some of society's most distressing and curious ailments.

Signs of sickness in the aura

Black inkspots

Black inkspots in the aura represent 'black holes' where there is no life. They indicate that a part of the person has died, for example, died of a broken heart. They simply mean that the person has been made numb by an experience. Adults who experienced abuse during their childhood, refugees who have witnessed the torture and death of friends and family, and car accident victims all exhibit inkspots in their auras. The placement of the inkspots in the aura is not relevant, as they can appear anywhere.

I recall a man in his mid-forties who sought my healing for a painful shoulder, which every healer he had previously gone to had treated unsuccessfully. On hearing this, I carefully scanned his aura. He sat opposite me and told the story of how this work-related injury had come about. I interrupted him and asked him how he had damaged his rib cage, approximately eighteen years ago. He thought deeply for a moment and then recalled a bumper-to-bumper car accident involving four cars. When I treated the internal bruising he had received during the accident, his shoulder healed immediately. I noticed that he still had auric inkspots over the chest area which must have been relating to something other than his shoulder. With a little coaxing, he admitted that he was dyslexic and had been the scapegoat of classmates and unforgiving teachers. He said, 'I deliberately can't remember my childhood.' I suggested that he undertake professional counselling to help him let go of this emotional pain.

Clouds

Grey clouds are an indicator of the development of organ disease or deterioration of joints. Red and maroon clouds indicate irritation and inflammation often due to the accumulation of unexpressed rage, sometimes originating in childhood. The person is usually unaware of the deep-seated cause.

A young woman came to me for healing of a continual throat ailment. A grey cloud engulfed her head, neck and shoulders. I gently nudged her emotions and challenged her inability to respond to the homoeopathic treatments that she had tried. She broke down and sobbed wretchedly in despair of being adopted and not knowing her origins.

Green slime

A murky lime green energy is seen in the aura when a person is taking drugs such as marijuana, heroin, psychiatric medication or consuming too much alcohol.

A single mother, embroiled in a very messy custody case for the care and control of her four-year-old son, sought healing from me to relieve the stress. On seeing the huge amount of green slime in her aura I questioned her about a drug habit. I described to her in graphic detail what I could see. She sat and stared at me blankly with no obvious answer to satisfy my concerns. Then she said, 'I've only been on medication for depression for the past fourteen years.' Well, the lecture that I had rehearsed in my head on the destructive nature of drug addictions quickly turned to fury when I discovered that doctors had done this to her. When I cautiously explained the extent of damage to her aura she, too, was outraged. Following several treatments by me, her psychiatrist reduced her medication.

Nets

Net-like patterns form grey criss-crosses over a specific part of the body and inhibit self-healing. Often people with this pattern in their aura are ignoring their health problems, hoping that they will go away. Most heavy smokers and heavy drinkers are perfect examples. Black mesh patterns indicate a more serious threat to health such as decay of organs. When a woman who was five months pregnant came to me for healing of a right knee injury, she was shocked when I insisted she contact her doctor immediately to check the heartbeat of the baby.

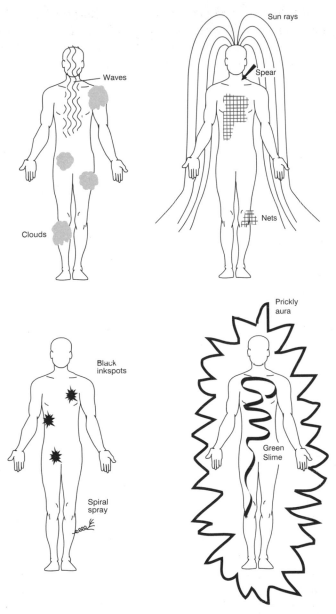

AURIC PATTERNS INDICATING HEALTH DISORDERS

A black mesh had woven its web over her womb. She was hospitalised that afternoon—her baby had died in the womb.

Prickly aura

A misty, spiky edged, pale grey cloud hugs the aura when a person is fearful. When someone is referred to see me by their doctor, often due to their religious beliefs, they are uncertain about the origins and intentions of spiritual healing. Within minutes of entering my consultation room, their aura takes on a pale grey prickly appearance.

A woman in her early fifties was referred to me by her doctor. She had been suffering with a pain in her stomach that x-rays could not locate. As I read the referral note, I noticed out of the corner of my eye the way in which she was sitting: still and rigid, as if she were frozen on the spot. The tell-tale pale grey cloud of fear was manifesting itself around her as she sat trembling. The doctor was kind enough to have informed me of her strict religious beliefs and her possible lack of acceptance of my form of healing. I coaxed her into closing her eyes and silently reciting the Lord's Prayer, as I proceeded with the healing. I could feel how secure she felt while in the embrace of her prayers. On the realisation that the pain had subsided, she kissed my hands and said, 'Christ was here with us, I know he was.'

Spears

Spears in the aura indicate pain in the area where they are present. It is not unusual to see dozens of spears in the aura of a person who has been involved in a major accident causing damage to the skeletal body. A man whom I treated many times for pain relief, had been crushed in a building accident at the age of nineteen. I'll never forget the state of his aura when I first began to treat him. Intense red and maroon spears littered his auric body showing how determined the body was to remain damaged. I used to throw my hands in the air because I truly didn't know where to begin. He would just laugh at me and say, 'Anywhere is fine with me.'

I have noticed that migraine sufferers, whose heads are always adorned with these painful spears, often have clouds around their neck, stomach or pelvis. When I remove the clouds from the aura, the spears instantly disappear. This leads me to conclude that the clouded area is the origin of the migraine.

Black spears can also be seen in an aura, indicating serious illness or disease.

Spiral sprays

These indicate an energy leak which inhibits the normal flow of the aura, causing coldness of the limbs. Circulatory disorders are associated with energy leaks. Many of my clients with multiple sclerosis experience energy leaks in their aura as the body begins to deteriorate. If I am able to seal the leak and restore the aura, while at the same time treat the cause of the disease, the person no longer experiences coldness in their limbs.

Sun rays

These are cream in colour and can be seen pouring like a fountain from the top of the head, down the entire body to the feet, when a person is overcoming a major catastrophe or chronic illness. Often when I have successfully helped my clients win the battle with cancer, a cream fountain appears at the top of the head washing the entire body with a new lease on life.

Waves

Wave-like patterns, short in length, and grey-blue in colour, are commonly associated with depression, anxiety attacks, fluid retention, angina, and colitis. I have noticed that the waves increase to the full length of the body when chronic fatigue, multiple sclerosis, Alzheimer's disease or Parkinson's disease are present.

The benefits of aura diagnosis

Auras, to me, are a vital part of physical and psychological diagnosis. They can be used to discover the cause of an ailment or to confirm its existence. My sister-in-law had suffered with a painful hip condition for a number of years. When conventional medicine failed to diagnose her, she sought an alternative diagnosis. She consulted my husband Paul, a highly respected Bowen Therapy practitioner, for treatment. They stood, casually discussing the matter for quite some time. As I breezed passed them I boldly interrupted and said, 'There's nothing wrong with the hip. According to your aura your foot has been throwing the hip out of alignment. Looks like it began in childhood.' She stared thoughtfully, recalling how often shoe repairs were required for the very foot that I had pointed to.

A number of my elderly clients complain of pain that conventional medicine says is psychosomatic. One dear old lady sought my healing for an eye condition. I noticed a red spear in her right hip and enquired as to the origin of the severe pain. She retorted, 'I did not tell you about my hip. So, why are you asking? Can you really see a pain there?' Apparently she had been examined by her family doctor and also by two specialists who all suggested the pain was imaginary. She was relieved when I found it without any previous information. When we returned to the reception area of my clinic, she loudly exclaimed to her husband that the pain was real.

One experience that I will never forget is an encounter I had with a cute three-year-old boy with big brown eyes and an olive complexion. His mother had consulted me because doctors were unable to advise her about her son's health, and each day she could see that he was becoming weaker. I assessed his aura and discovered a serious blood disorder, possibly poisonous. She outlined the numerous unsuccessful tests he had had in an attempt to locate the cause. When I suggested that she ask her doctor to do blood tests of a chemical nature, she confirmed what I expected—the doctor had told her that she was over-reacting. So, I suggested that she go to a doctor outside her local area or better still, a hospital. As we talked, I noticed how the child clung to his mother like a baby monkey. When I questioned this, she explained that he was possessive and she had been unable to wean him from the breast. As I pursued my line of advice she became convinced to follow it. But, I never heard from her again.

To my surprise, and delight, almost three years later she brought a sick friend to a healing circle that I was conducting. Moving towards me, she said in an enquiring manner, 'Do you remember me and my son?' Of course I did. I had sent a piece of my heart with him for good luck, so how could I forget him. Introducing her ailing friend to me she remarked to her, 'This is the lady who saved my son's life.' Following my advice earnestly, she coerced a doctor into finally discovering the nature of the poison. Apparently, some years prior to the child's birth she had had a silicon breast implant. Although breast feeding was successful for the first two and a half years of her son's life, during the last six months silicon had leaked into her breast milk, and consequently into her son's body with potentially tragic results.

Silvana, a young woman, tells her own story of a brush with what could have become life-threatening.

Silvana's story

I went to see Judith at the Mind, Body and Spirit festival in November, 1995. I didn't know why I went to see her, only that I'd been drawn back to her, every time I went past her stall. She drew my aura and picked up that I had stress all around my sexual organs. I thought it unusual and went to get it checked. The doctors discovered I had the third stage of development of cervical cancer. I was stunned, as I'd had an annual pap smear the past five years, all of which had come back supposedly normal.

There is nothing more entertaining to me than a sceptic. Frequently I am confronted with questions such as, 'Can you really see auras?' Being accustomed to people's sceptical questions all my life, I always welcome an opportunity to prove a point and usually reveal some deep, dark mystery buried in the person's aura and then watch their awareness and acceptance expand instantly. Here Norm Way tells his own story of conversion.

Norm's story

Because of some health problems I have experienced lately, my wife Pat suggested that I have an aura reading and health analysis with Judith on her recent visit to the area. Being an open-minded sceptic, I duly went along to see her.

To my absolute amazement, after a few minutes Judith told me my whole medical history. By simply looking at my aura Judith was able to diagnose every illness in my body, from a thirty-year-old knee injury to more recent chest and asthma problems related to toxic poisons which are still in my body from being gassed with methyl bromide at work. She also picked up a heart murmur which I had been aware of and a thyroid problem.

Doctors tell me there is nothing wrong with my knee though at times it causes severe pain, and all they can do for my chest is prescribe a Ventolin® puffer—giving no credence to the existence of the gases still lingering in the body. Judith was able to recommend various treatments for each condition, which I am now pursuing.

Often at major new age shows where I produce an aura drawing and analysis approximately every ten minutes, I come across people who delight in having their aura drawn, but who are not always open to what it exposes. Raylene Swain was one person who discovered that an aura reveals the truth. Here in her own words Raylene openly shares the events which led her to believe the message of her aura.

Raylene's story

Last year at the Body Health and Harmony Show, I had my aura read by Judith Collins. Part of that reading highlighted an area more or less above to below my breasts, and Judith told me to be very careful and listen to my body because there was a problem in that area. I laughed and said, 'Not likely, as everyone in my family has died of some kind of cancer, and I do not smoke so would not have lung cancer!'

A few weeks later I had a referral to Prince Charles Hospital to see about my breathing as I was having problems, and the doctor had picked up a noise. This noise was discovered to be a mid-systolic clic at apex (a malfunction with the valve leading to my heart), whereas the breathing problem was nothing but stress.

People never cease to be amazed at what an aura can reveal about them and their state of health. Year after year at major festivals, I am visited by enthusiasts who seek to know themselves better through opening to self-awareness via their aura. Some people return to me regularly for an evaluation of their health and personal progress.

The trauma caused by mis-diagnosis

A middle-aged woman came to me in a state of emotional shock and in desperate need of stabilising. She had lost her voice for three months and her breathing had become dangerously shallow. When I placed my hands on her upper back at the commencement of the healing, her body shook with fear and tears flowed down her cheeks. Searching the aura for traces of physical and sexual abuse, I found chronic loss and separation. Instinctively, I knew these pent-up emotions were making her ill. With a concerted effort, I opened her higher mental auric layer and connected it to mine, in order to bring her inspiration and comfort. As it quickly filtered through the various layers of her aura, the healing penetrated her body and caused her emotions to swell. Placing my hand on her chest I applied healing to the stress in her throat, chest and stomach. This was followed by a wailing scream from the woman that echoed down the corridors in the clinic. My staff were puzzled as to what I was doing. The woman sat up and wept on my shoulder for a full twenty minutes. She revealed how her husband had run off with another woman and she had been deserted and hurt on all fronts. Further to this, she unveiled a sorry account of exposure to insincere hands of healing.

She had attended an introductory evening to Reiki healing, at her daughter's request, in the hope that a cure would be found for what ailed her. The facilitator of the programme selected the woman as a demonstration model. She lay on the massage table, closed her eyes and expected to feel the relaxing ray of energy which had been so eloquently described.

Instead, one of the healers, who had a fertile imagination and no regard for the consequence, dramatically stood back and said to her, 'You are in desperate need of healing. There is a ten metre etheric python snake moving through your aura, attempting to suffocate you. If we don't put it to rest, it will take your life.' She didn't know what to believe. Could it be true? She didn't know enough about the healing modality to tell. Consequently, when her daughter brought her to me for treatment, the woman shook with psychological fear.

The cause of her ailment lay not with an imaginary snake but with the fact that her parents had been killed in a car accident when she was four years old and she was reared by her doting grandmother, who died when she was twelve years old. She was then placed in the care of her aunt, but two days after her eighteenth birthday the aunt died of bowel cancer. Fortunately she fell into the comfort of her lover's arms and they soon married. But after twenty-five years he ran away with her life-long girlfriend. Finally, her body had had enough and shut down to protect itself.

If the healer had truly been able to see and read her aura, he would never have made such a traumatic statement and tainted the purity of Reiki healing.

Auric diagnosis through etheric hands

Another means of detecting the health of an aura is through hands-on healing. By scanning approximately eight centimetres above and around a body with his or her hands, a healer locates variations in body temperature which indicate overactive and underactive parts of the physical body. This allows the healer to accurately diagnose sluggish, blocked and inflamed organs. Furthermore, when a healer is compassionately attuned to his or her client, their auras combine within minutes to allow the healing energy to transfer from the healer to the client. As a result, a healer's etheric hands are stimulated and penetrate the physical auric layer of the client, giving both the sense of surgery taking place. Up to forty-eight hours later, the physical layer of the aura displays the healing that has taken place.

I personally use the etheric scanning technique to confirm what I see in an aura and also to locate disorders which may be beginning but which have not yet manifested themselves in the aura. The combination of this technique and aura diagnosis permits me to diagnose accurately.

Group healing

Because of my very busy healing schedule, whenever I work around the country or in large cities, I conduct a healing circle, which is just as successful as my private healing consultations, to allow large numbers of people to gain access to my healing skills. There are usually between fifty to one hundred people involved. I seat them in close proximity to each other, and ask them to hold hands to encourage their auras to blend into one communal aura. Within three minutes their auras have blended. I then attune myself to a divine healing force and send a beam of energy through the group aura by placing my hands on the head of each individual in the circle. It's an amazing experience that never ceases to amaze the recipients, and it encourages me in my work.

The following extract from a report by Irene Phipps, published in the 1995 Spring edition of the *Judith Collins Newsletter*, tells of the benefits gained from a healing circle.

> When Judith's hands rested on Trudy's shoulders during the healing she immediately felt a flow of energy and relief from long-term back pain. The pain relief so amazed her, and the healing experience was so profound, that she went to Judith for additional healing.

Trudy's friend also benefited from the powerful healing energy that night. She was suffering from a painful knee condition which had been diagnosed as needing surgery. After the healing, the pain ceased and when examined by her doctor the knee showed no sign of damage, making the proposed operation unnecessary.

Auric diagnosis aids medical diagnosis

While working in Western Australia, I met a lady who had been diagnosed and treated for diabetes. She was in chronic pain and feared the long-term effects of the disease, so she sought my help. To my surprise I was unable to find any sign of diabetes. Instead, a faulty liver was reigning havoc over the other organs. Following the treatment I armed her with a list of questions to ask her doctors.

Returning to my hotel room that evening, I sincerely pondered on how many people are being treated for misdiagnosed ailments. Too many of my clients with cancer, chronic fatigue, multiple sclerosis and other chronic illnesses, tell me stories of their one to two years of pain, discomfort and exhaustive tests, prior to being accurately diagnosed.

A middle-aged man suffering from bone cancer consulted me as a last resort. Through the torturous pain of radiation therapy, he had come to recognise the seriousness of his illness. The first time I treated him, with my hands on his body and within his physical and etheric auric layers, I could feel his pain and fear. His aura revealed that the cancer's primary source had not been located or medically treated. When he verbally confirmed my suspicions, I examined the aura carefully and hit the jackpot. I produced a diagram for his doctors and they addressed the problem promptly.

Does this leave me frustrated with conventional medicine? No, but I dare to imagine how an aura-seeing medical profession could make the process of diagnosis so much more accurate and efficient.

A strong, healthy looking twenty-year-old requested that I try to heal his brain tumour. It had affected his eyesight and occasionally his speech. He was a bright university student, charged with the youthful excitement of the future, and he had no vision of impending death, despite the dominance that the tumour was exhibiting with its murky grey cloud and maroon and black spears. I took up his challenge and together we worked for his improved health. By the fourth treatment, I noticed the aura displaying grey flecks around the location of the tumour, indicating that it was decaying. Thrilled with the result, I did not hesitate in sharing my findings with him. The tumour was dying. Now, it was only a matter of time and he would be free of it. A couple of months later his father came to thank me. A medical scan of his son's head had revealed that the tumour had gone.

Fortunately more and more people in the nursing profession are becoming aware of natural, instinctive alternatives to conventional medical treatments. I have taught many nurses and other caring individuals throughout Australia to see and feel auras, as well as how to attune to and use the techniques of auric diagnosis and spiritual healing. Also, to my delight conventional health practitioners are awakening to other levels of knowing. In 1994, Dr Bronwyn Neubecker (BDSc.) consulted me. She had this to say:

> Your gift is extraordinary and just goes to show that some people really can make use of more than the mere ten per cent of the brain that science concludes that the rest of us get by functioning on. If only science could come to understand better and make use of what you seem to be able to do so easily, it would be a wonderful diagnostic aid for many conditions, both physical as well as psychological/emotional in nature. There is much to gain from taking an holistic view to diagnosis and treatment in the area of health and medicine.

> I see no reason why the alternatives cannot be selec-
> tively used in conjunction with mainstream medicine. It is
> the patient who loses out if either method is unfairly dis-
> missed as not being of any merit.

As individuals take a stand against environmental pollution and the invasive pain of war and hunger, communal awareness of natural resources prevails. Natural health care will be among the great strides forward. I sincerely believe that a time will come when conventional medicine and natural medicine will lovingly hold hands, because they both agree that prevention is better than cure.

When I have been called to treat patients in hospital, I have always found that doctors and their staff are generally polite, if not open-minded. I like to think that I merely complement their vast knowledge and work with them for the benefit of the patient.

A client of mine's husband had a debilitating accident during a parade in his local town. On admission to hospital he was examined by medical staff who described his condition as very serious and placed him in an intensive care ward for ongoing supervision. His comatose state inhibited their analysis and treatment.

My client invited me to treat her husband. On entering the intensive care unit, I could feel all eyes on me as medical staff, aware of the role I was to play, gathered around. I assessed the damage as displayed in the physical layer of the patient's aura and explained my findings to his family and medical attendants. Noticing a blood clot on the brain, I lay my hands on his head and healed it. His astral aura revealed that he was frightened of regaining consciousness for fear of physical disablement. After explaining this predicament to my audience, I quickly set about quelling the emotional turmoil of the aura. On completion of my diagnosis and treatment I announced that the patient would regain consciousness within the next few hours, which he did. When he regained consciousness he asked for me by description, 'the doctor with the long blonde hair'. His etheric aura had subconsciously recorded who had relieved his suffering, then supplied his conscious mind with the memory.

Visible healing effects in the aura

Over the years I have helped many people towards good health simply by assessing their auric vibrations and steering them in the right direction. In my healing profession I have had the opportunity to witness how medication and natural healing modalities affect the body, through monitoring their progress in the auras of my clients. I have been able to see how quick and effective they may or may not be. I have also noted that different people resonate to different natural healing modalities. To complicate matters further, you may have three different ailments. One will respond to acupuncture, one to herbs and the other to homoeopathy. Hence, I frequently have clients who consult me just for direction towards the most appropriate means of healing for a specific problem.

The following natural healing modalities and medications can be used successfully in conjunction with auric diagnosis to relieve and eradicate many illnesses.

Acupuncture

Acupuncture is recognised as the world's oldest medical system, dating back to the time before Christ. It was brought from China to the West by seventeeth-century Jesuit priests. It works with the flow of ch'i, a subtle energy that flows through fourteen clearly defined channels in the human body known as meridians. Thin needles are inserted at specific meridian points to regulate the body's flow of energy via the meridians and the chakras, in order to facilitate healing of the physical body and the aura. Long after the needles have been removed, chakras and meridians display the healing effects. I have noticed that acupuncture is particularly effective with stroke victims as it realigns the vital auric layer, which assists the person in regaining their health.

My mother suffered a mild stroke which left her partially disabled. Her doctors prescribed physiotherapy treatment but it failed her. My father suggested chiropractic treatment but it, too, failed her. On my return from a lecture tour, I assessed her aura and announced that acupuncture was the key. After only eight treatments my mother was completely cured.

Australian Bush Flower Essences

These homoeopathic drops play an integral role in healing the mind, body and spirit. Medication, while eradicating most symptoms, does not always address the cause. Furthermore, its side effects can be seen in the aura for many years, clogging systems and causing a sluggish response in organs, especially the pancreas, liver and kidneys. Some years ago a friend of mine convinced my husband to undertake a course with her in the homoeopathic remedies known as Australian Bush Flower Essences. They returned from their venture greatly impressed and brimming over with newly acquired resources for their individual healing practices. I could see by their auras that they had indeed discovered something remarkable. As each bottle of medication was eagerly unpacked I could see a vibrant energy emanating within and without it. I was hooked too.

As fate would have it, it was not long before Ian White, founder of the essences, made his way to my door for spiritual healing. We spoke about his work for a short while, during which time our auras cemented a lasting friendship through mutual respect.

It didn't take me long to realise that many of these essences have beneficial effects on the aura and that they work well in conjunction with my healing work. Consequently, numerous essence bottles line the shelves of my clinic's dispensary. Although I have never done Ian's course, I frequently refer to the essences. I simply glance at my client's aura and then scan the dispensary shelves using the etheric energy of my left hand to match my client's auric vibrations with the appropriate essence. This system of reference has fascinated Ian for years, not only because I always choose what he himself would prescribe, but because I have been able to describe to him additional healing potentialities of a number of essences.

I regularly use the following essences in conjunction with my healing sessions because of their very strong resonance to the human aura:

COGNIS ESSENCE

Cognis essence aligns the physical and lower mental layers of the aura for co-ordination of mind and body, which in turn leads to greater focus.

I noticed that when my niece was studying for her final school exams, she was totally overwhelmed. The lower mental auric layer was imbalanced, and this essence worked wonders for her. Now I recommend it to all anxious students facing exams.

CONFID ESSENCE

Confid essence affects the astral and lower mental auric layers, causing them to merge, giving a balance of thought and emotion, to produce confidence and self-empowerment.

A young man with a speech impediment who found it difficult to express himself during interviews came to me for help. He had been unemployed for several years and his confidence was very low. I focused on healing his panic attacks and suggested he use Confid to help him to overcome his general nervousness. He took it several times, several hours ahead of his interview, and succeeded in completing the interview without nervous fumbles. Although he didn't get the job, he made the grade with a new-found confidence.

DYNAMIS ESSENCE

Dynamis essence affects the vital layer of the aura. It stimulates and expands it, leaving the person feeling revitalised. I have found it of value to people suffering with chronic fatigue as it helps them to get through the day.

EMERGENCY ESSENCE

Emergency essence is always in my handbag. It stimulates the physical auric layer and causes the body to come into alignment with the balance of the etheric body. Hence floating germs and viruses are easily eradicated before they really take hold. At the first sign of a sore throat, blocked nasal passages or head tension due to a long and tiring schedule, I place a few drops under my tongue and I bounce back.

HEARTSONG ESSENCE

Heartsong essence brings the physical, vital and astral layers of the aura into harmony, encouraging greater self-expression.

A middle-aged lady, feeling trapped by her domestic life, took the essence on my recommendation. Days later she reported how she had aired bottled up feelings towards her family and felt inspired to go in search of her own creative talents. She took up ceramics and enrolled in a singing class. I had no doubt that her life-force had expanded.

MEDIATION ESSENCE

Meditation essence aligns the lower mental auric layer, encouraging its receptivity to the spiritual vibrations which filter through the higher mental auric layer. I recommend this essence to my chronically ill clients who must relax and let go in order to heal themselves.

RELATIONSHIP ESSENCE

Relationship essence addresses the aura's emotional knots, and helps to untangle trying and non-communicative relationships, creating a degree of harmony. A woman in her second marriage was encountering the same difficulties as she did in her first marriage. After she and her husband took the drops for two weeks, I noticed that their astral and vital auric layers were relaxed and flowing. The couple reported the same feelings.

SOLARIS ESSENCE

Solaris essence stimulates the aura's electromagnetic energy field, causing it to sort and sift any foreign energy particles which may cause damage, such as gamma rays, microwaves and x-rays. It is known to bring old sunburn damage to the surface and cure it. One young woman took it to help combat side effects from radiation treatment of her cancer. Within days a five-year-old bikini sunburn line surfaced.

TRAVEL ESSENCE

Travel essence aligns and strengthens the vibrations of all layers of the aura, preventing travel sickness and offsetting vertigo.

I love this essence because it prevents me from suffering from jetlag on long flights. I suggested it to my brother and sister-in-law when they flew from Australia to meet me in England. As they walked through the gate at Heathrow Airport, they looked refreshed and raring to go, whereas their fellow passengers resembled zombies.

Bowen therapy

This is perhaps the natural healing modality that impresses me the most. It was developed in Geelong, in the state of Victoria in Australia, by the late Tom Bowen, and is now taught worldwide. A Bowen therapist gently touches the soft tissue, stimulating the body's energy flow, empowering it to heal itself. One simple movement sends changes rippling through the body. A stiff neck can be released within minutes. Menstrual pain dissolves within minutes too. Ailments such as tennis elbow and frozen shoulder really benefit from this therapy. The dramatic change can instantly be seen in the aura as debilitating patterns fade, then disappear.

Homoeopathy

This method of healing calls on the body's own substantial reserves to heal itself. The theory behind it, 'like can cure like', is contrary to established medical practice. A substance which can produce symptoms in large doses can cure similar symptoms in minute doses. For example, May Apple in excess causes profuse and foul smelling diarrhoea. But in a homoeopathic preparation it is called Podophyllum and is used to cure the same symptoms.

A homoeopath uses a potentising machine to create dosages so minute that not a single molecule of the original substance can be detected in the actual medicine. Potentising is a system of dilution and succussion which releases the energy of the original substance. Several drops of this tasteless remedy under the tongue can take effect in most cases almost immediately.

Over fifteen years ago I consulted the well-known Sydney homoeopath, Alan Jones, to address my allergic reaction to

smoke. This affliction not only clogged my breathing apparatus, it also produced painful sores in the nostrils. Alan dis-
pensed a homoeopathic remedy and said that the allergy
would subside in about two weeks. However, unbeknown to
me at the time, my aura resonates strongly towards this healing modality and I was cured within four days and have not
suffered since.

When a practitioner makes an accurate diagnosis, as seen in
my own case above, ill health can vanish almost spontaneously. Homoeopathy engages the vibrations of the physical,
vital, astral and lower mental levels of the aura in an attempt
to bring them into alignment to meet the needs of the material body. It vibrates to the very essence of our life-force and
can have a powerful impact.

Meditation and prayer

When a person meditates or prays, circular patterns of violet
and cream light cascade like a fountain from the top of the
head, spilling over the face. The vital and astral auric layers
expand into the lower and higher mental levels, opening the
psyche to a different awareness. The physical layer adjusts
into the etheric layer to capture all sensations.

The etheric layer of the aura may separate from the rest of
the aura, facilitating what is known as an out-of-body experience.

Spiritual healing

This form of healing requires a healer to be in communication with the spirit realm so that divine healing energy may
flow through their auric spirit layers and into the hands of the
healer. The energy usually creates a warm tingling effect in
the client's body as it addresses the cause of the affliction. It
works via the vital and physical layers of the aura, causing the

physical body to align with the patterns of well-being in the etheric auric body.

Spiritual healing and homoeopathy have a working relationship. In some instances, the two methods combined have brought about some simply wonderful results.

Therapeutic aromatherapy

Aromatherapy is the application of essential oils to open the body to healing through stimulating its senses. For example, jasmine uplifts and yarrow soothes. Essential oils represent the soul of the plant from which they are extracted and are the most concentrated form of herbal energy, with powerful antiseptic, antibiotic and antiviral properties. They are used externally in the gentle process of aromatherapeutic massage and through inhalations. My husband Paul, who is also an aromatherapist, combines essential oils for localised application by his clients. He has a blend of oil to help women during childbirth; a blend to relieve skeletal pain; a blend to release muscular tension; a blend to relieve varicose veins— the list seems endless. When the family is choked up with the flu virus, he burns lavender oil, a decongestant, to clear the breathing passages and aid sleep. Five drops of rosemary oil when added to warm bath water soothes tired and strained muscles.

Essential oils stimulate the aura by exciting its electromagnetic particles through the physical senses. They can activate the vital auric layer and give it new vigour. They can calm and balance the senses by encouraging the physical, vital and astral layers of the aura to release pent-up stress and to harmonise.

Death in the aura

Once in a while a person who is resigned to death is ushered into my clinic against his or her will by a well-meaning relative or friend. Generally their aura shows grey and pink tiered waves, interlaced with pastel green. Working with chronic illness as I do, death frequently parades in front of me. However, it is not until the vital level of the aura is finely outlined with a grey shimmer of light that I accept death as inevitable. To spiritually prepare the client to enter peacefully through death's door and to ease the emotions of their carer, I consent to proceed with healing.

When a person is resigned to death it is a challenge to know how to best attend them. I assess their auric patterns and then listen to their conversation to ascertain their resignation. A young woman was diagnosed with lung cancer and within a few months the cancer had spread. Accepting her doctor's advice, she prepared for the worst and set about arranging household affairs so that her husband could cope with the care of their children after her death.

A devoted friend brought her to me and I immediately set about healing her. Within twenty minutes she had regained the use of her paralysed left arm. A three-month-long pain in her throat subsided and her breathing was smoother and painless. Her skin tone also revitalised. I was so excited that I gave her every chance of recovery and told her so.

Unfortunately, I was unaware that she had only consulted me to appease her friend. Although she appreciated what I had done for her, there was no commitment to continue the healing. Instead she talked incessantly of the plans she had to make to clear her way to die in peace. The grey and maroon patterns in her aura showed how firmly she held onto the victim and self-pity mentality. So I knew I could not divert her course of action.

Some years ago a middle-aged woman brought her elderly father to see me. He had been diagnosed as having bowel and bladder cancer and was refusing all forms of treatment. Before she introduced him, she begged me to reason with him and entice him to want to live. The withered old man shuffled into my office. His face shone with contentment, which was no wonder as his aura displayed the colourful ripples of inter-twined grey, pale pink, salmon pink, pale blue and maroon, indicating his determination to die.

It was a wonderful healing session. I can remember that he talked continually of his love for his departed wife and how they had been together since the age of sixteen and they had had a happy marriage for sixty-three years, until she passed away. He explained how tired he was of living alone. Certainly, he loved his children and grandchildren, who had all grown to adulthood. He had done his duty by his family. He felt that each day seemed longer and more empty, and he had simply grown tired of living. My heart went out to this man. I could see in his aura that he was not throwing in the towel, so to speak. In his heart of hearts a signal beamed telling him to let go of life and fade away. I simply told his daughter to untie the apron strings, the same way she had asked her parents to do so, when she was a fledgling adult and wanted so much to be free.

I learnt so much in the half hour that I spent with this wonderful man. As tears came to my eyes, he leaned forward, touched my hand and said, 'If life serves you as well as it has served me and mine, you will have been blessed.' Unassumingly, he prepared my way for an increase of work with the elderly, and helped me to understand the morals and values of their era, and to comprehend their pioneering strength and tenacity.

I was given the pleasure by one of my clients to hold his hand as he relaxed to welcome death. The pulse of his blood and shallow breathing were his only signs of life. He was physically still, and wandering in and out of consciousness, but I could read his thoughts through his aura. The astral layer was swirling furiously as it replayed the memories of his life that would assure him of completion. The vital layer was depleting in colour and vibrance rapidly, showing that death would soon come. The etheric layer sucked up the physical layer in a cone-shaped vacuum which spun over and around the stomach area. Out of the corner of my right eye, I saw a colourful spirit figure standing opposite me. It was his son who had died during adolescence. As the process of letting go of life intensified, the etheric layer of the aura gently sank into his physical body and then, within seconds, rose high above the bed. It was at this point I knew that he was having an out-of-body experience—the self-recognition phase of retirement and transition from life.

The whole process was like watching a factory shut down for the weekend. The building secured, the lights turned off, the windows and doors bolted. Everything ground to a stand-still as the employees headed off home.

Death can be such a positive experience for those who have an understanding of the spirit realm and believe that death is merely a transition process from the material life to the spirit life.

A tall, stout man, who was riddled with cancer and fearful of dying asked me to help him accept death. So I set about explaining the layers of the aura and how they function from birth to death. I further explained the spirit realm who care and watch over us. He soon realised that no one dies alone. From the moment you lose consciousness your mind is in the loving hold of the spirit realm. On my next visit to Western Australia, his wife informed me of his death just weeks prior to my arrival. She said, 'at the end, he was not afraid, only sorry that they had to part after forty happy years of marriage.' A true believer, she knew they would meet again when her time to die arrived.

6

THE LIVING AURA
OF NATURE

A fool sees not the same tree that a wise man sees.

William Blake

Plants and trees have a balanced aura that provides a life-giving force to those who share their space. Beginning the day in attunement with nature creates well-being. The crisp, fresh air of a country morning heightens primal senses and awakens the human connection to nature. Ten minutes of this earthy essence is enough to clear the cobwebs from the mind and set in motion a chain reaction throughout the aura, cleansing and restoring it to balance. The earthy essence of which I speak is the balance of nature itself. Many people are not fortunate enough to live in the country, so a morning walk or a swim, a bicycle or horse ride, an outdoor meditation, half an hour of gardening, a hot air balloon ride, or a Tai Chi workout in your garden or local park, are just a few of the many ways to embrace nature and enhance your aura.

The healing nature of trees

The yellow gold and soft green colours of the aura of a mature, healthy tree outline its canopy, while more subtle darker green shades highlight the trunk. These basic colours are a reflection of the tree's balance with nature. The bright, glittering colours of the human aura which are produced by the emotions are not present in the auras of trees and plants, as they manage to maintain an even balance.

A tree's aura remains perfect in shape at almost all times, altering only when human, animal or bird interference threatens to destroy its balance. In self-defence, the tree withdraws the auric energy of its canopy into the trunk, as if to preserve its life at all costs. Disease appears as muddy blotches or a fraying of auric colour around the outer perimeter of the leaves, highlighting a problem in the physiology of the tree. Streaks of murky green-brown in a tree's aura indicate a problem in the root or trunk.

Not so long ago it was trendy to hug a tree. This environmental embrace, in reality, did more for the individual person than the tree. A community locked into varying patterns of survival, unconsciously produces a social aura that floats several metres above the roof tops of houses. A mature tree's canopy sits high above this finely interwoven, multi-coloured, collective aura of society. Tall, healthy trees are beyond the human communal and social auras and therefore remain relatively unaffected by it. Of course there is atmospheric pollution for trees to contend with but, overall, a tree's aura remains more in balance than a human's does. A tree's roots are secured by the earth and its canopy sways in the freedom of the sky. This two-way connection gives trees the very balance which those on a spiritual path strive.

St Francis of Assisi is perhaps one of the most famous environmentalists in the Christian tradition. In his endeavour to reunite other human beings with Creation, he observed and reconnected with its beauty and simplicity and found the wonder of God in all living things, as we see here in his 'Praise of Created Things' or 'Canticle of the Sun', as it is best known.

Most High, Omnipotent, Good Lord,

Thine be the praise, the glory, the honour and all benediction.

To Thee alone, Most High, they are due, and no man is worthy to mention Thee.

Be Thou praised, my Lord, with all Thy creatures, above all Brother Sun who gives the day and lightens us therewith.

And he is beautiful and radiant with great splendour, of Thee, Most High, he bears similitude.

Be Thou praised, my Lord, of Sister Moon and the stars, in the heaven hast Thou formed them, clear and precious and comely.

Be Thou praised, my Lord, of Brother Wind, and of the air, and the cloud, and of fair and all weather, by which Thou givest to Thy creatures sustenance.

Be Thou praised, my Lord, of Sister Water, which is much useful and humble and precious and pure.

Be Thou praised, my Lord, of Brother Fire, by which Thou hast lightened the night, and he is beautiful and joyful and robust and strong.

Be Thou praised, my Lord, of our sister Mother Earth, which sustains and hath us in rule, and produces diverse fruits with coloured flowers and herbs.

My fascination and appreciation of nature began when I was very young. On a school excursion to an orphanage one hot summer's day, a few classmates and I took shelter under the sprawling limbs of an old pine tree. Immediately, I noticed that the rays of the sun could not pierce the shade created by the tree, nor could a summer shower when it broke. There we sat, protected by this huge umbrella, grumbling about the boring excursion and gossiping as young girls do. As the conversation grew kinder, I witnessed a steady change occurring in my classmates' auras. Looking about for the trigger, I saw beads of energy strung together like a string of pearls, spilling droplets of energy into their auras. The tree's aura was acting like a cleansing agent. Spontaneously, I thought of a television advertisement for Lux washing flakes and how they make everything whiter and brighter. Soon, my intuitive gaze caught the attention of my friends and they, with their silly remarks, distracted me. This was the first time that I had consciously observed the healing power of trees, although I did not realise its significance at the time.

It was not until I found a cat on my way home from school some months later, whose rear end had been maimed by explosive fireworks, that I learnt the true healing value of trees. For protection from the scorching rays of the sun, I placed the cat under the canopy of a pine tree. The poor little thing must have been no more than six months old. As I sat stroking its head pondering on the least painful way to carry it home to my doting mother, again, I saw beads of energy emanating from a tree. The energy was connecting with the cat. Something prompted me to sit very still and watch the whole process for over an hour. Each time the tree's green and yellow beads of energy spilt over into the cat's aura, the animal grew slightly stronger as the fear in its aura dispersed. Never again did I take the landscape for granted. When I was troubled during my adolescence I sought the refuge of public parks where old pine trees stood.

My understanding of the healing nature of trees means that I take great care when selecting a tree to plant in my garden. I never rush into a nursery and sift through their stock for a tree or shrub that would fit the spot in my garden. Instead, I assess the plants, aura by aura, and dare to play the role of matchmaker with nature. Within two weeks of moving into my home twelve years ago, I single-handedly planted forty radiata pine trees, which today tower high above my rooftop, creating a corridor of healing and a wall of privacy.

When you hear a person being referred to as having a 'green thumb', generally their aura has a range of earth-connected colours such as browns and greens, which easily exchange a sense of sharing and nurturing with their garden. Such an exchange is understood and welcomed by nature and plants respond with a healthy vibrance.

Like people and animals, trees have individual personalities and roles which can easily be defined by their unique auric vibrations. When I see a tree I view it in all its glory. I see the earth connection housed within its trunk shining like an internal lantern. I understand the melodic echoes of its auric rhythms as it grows in attunement with Creation.

At times, trees have revealed to me what they have witnessed during their growth. When I was about ten years old my family went on a picnic to the Royal Botanic Gardens in Sydney. As the summer sun pierced our lightweight clothing, we sought shelter beneath a large tree. My mother laid down a blanket and set about serving the picnic feast, while I skipped along talking to the trees and birds. After lunch I leaned back on the tree's trunk, closed my eyes and said a warm hello. My mind was immediately filled with the vision of two young children from the previous century who had also befriended the tree. A boy had been left to care for his polio-crippled sister while his parents wandered about the parkland. I could feel the healing vibrations of the tree as it sought to heal the defenceless young girl. With that I rolled on to my side and gently kissed the bark of the tree in recognition of its contribution to her life.

An unpleasant encounter with an old tree also springs to my mind. It was near the ruined convict prison at Port Arthur, Tasmania. My husband and I had taken a few days off from a conference to tour the island. Our interest in history enticed us to visit the old convict sites. We quickly parked and alighted from the hire car. Before I could take more than ten steps from the car my aura shivered and vibrated, sending me into a dramatic frenzy, crowding my voice and flooding my eyes with endless tears. My husband ushered me to the car as I babbled out the torment of so many lost souls. It took me twenty drawn-out minutes to regain my composure. My husband suggested that I seek the refuge of a huge tree nearby while he went through the ruins.

As I approached the tree at the bottom of the hill I could see its vast canopy overshadowing a large grassland. Its healing emanations drew me closer. As I stepped under the canopy, my aura flew into a frenzy once again. I wobbled back and forth, quite unstable on my feet. People were looking at me as if I were insane. I desperately tried to control myself, but to no avail. Visions of blood-stained ground and wailing sounds locked my mind into the horrors of the reality of the place. I managed to break myself free of the tree's auric tug, and ran sobbing up the hill. On reflection, I realise that the tree was attempting to heal the negativity of the area, not to attack me. It was unfortunate that, at that time, my intuitive senses were open and unguarded, so I copped the lot!

The healing qualities of individual trees

The list of trees below, whose energy is of great value to human beings, is based on my personal observations and experiences related to me by friends, relatives and my aura course participants.

BIRCH
Birch restores and balances human traits.

ELM
Elm enhances strength of character.

EUCALYPTUS
Eucalypt enhances personal strengths during a crisis.

FRUIT

Fruit trees open you to a sense of new growth of life.

MAGNOLIA

Magnolia stimulates the purity of Self.

MAPLE

Maple aids in the preparation of major change.

OAK

Oak enhances wisdom for self-analysis and self-counselling.

PINE

Pine cleanses and balances by absorbing negativity.

POPLAR

Poplar replenishes the vital auric energy flow.

WILLOW

Willow alleviates head tension and confusion.

To gain full benefit from any tree, first make certain that it is taller than the rooftop of a single-storey house. Secondly, be prepared to sit under its canopy for one or more hours. You may choose to place a rug and cushion on the ground, and lie back and read a book, or even better, to meditate. Either way, a relaxed, welcoming attitude encourages the tree to respond to the needs advertised in your aura.

Primitive cultures, whose great insight into nature was gathered through daily existence, used, and passed on, their vast knowledge down through the ages to sustain themselves.

My knowledge, too, has been acquired through observation and interaction. In particular, the auric healing qualities of different trees has been my focus.

Animal auras

The many family trips to the zoo during my childhood exposed me to the auras of a wide selection of animals. I remember being overwhelmed by it all. Eventually, I became aware of the differing colours and patterns of the animals' individual auras. Still, today, it is the platypus that fascinates me the most because its aura is very similar to that of the cat, despite the differences between their habitats and function in nature. If I could have a platypus as a pet, I wonder if it would purr, sit on my knee and demand attention!

As a child, monkeys never interested me because their auras were just as emotionally congested as their human keepers. It was the stately giraffe that caught my attention with the claret and pale blue auric glow about its head, advertising its sensitivity, yet self-empowered nature. The humble camel won my heart forever, with its auric mix of brown indicating practicality and durability; apricot, loyal companionship; and red, creative expression. Camels are one of the few animals that don't absorb their keeper's aura into their own. This means that the camel is master of its own destiny, unlike horses who, too often, not only absorb the human aura, but are also intent on sharing their keeper's pain. On reflection I have always been attracted to animals who are akin to my own nature, free thinking and independent.

Animals have a more basic array of colours in their auras than humans do. Most are compatible with humankind and this is felt in the bonding which occurs at an auric level. The physical and etheric layers of the human aura attune with the animal first, then the vital and astral layers engage with the animal's aura and a loyal bond is formed. This not only facilitates the balancing and restoration of the human aura, but can also stabilise blood pressure, nervous conditions and emotional disorders. The emotional supportive service they offer to humans is due to their earthiness via their primal link with nature. It is this compatibility that allows us to domesticate a large number of wild animals. Some animals, such as cats and dogs, are more compatible with humans than other animals.

The auric benefits of keeping cats and dogs

Just as some people are attracted to gardens, some are attracted to pets. The domestication of cats and dogs has helped to heal the emotional vulnerability that comes with being human. These savage, yet cute creatures are able to love and serve their keepers with the utmost loyalty. The strongest and most vibrant auras in the cat family belong to the cheetah and the jaguar, while in the dog family the strongest aura belongs to the Labrador.

A dog's aura is a mixture of browns, tans, pinks and midgreens and represents loving servitude. The cat's aura is a mixture of greens, blues, pinks and apricot, representing a loving, independent individual. This is the fundamental difference in the relationship a keeper has with their dog or cat. Although their auras function differently, both cats and dogs have the ability to restore or renew a human aura when a person is suffering from shock, depression or fear. However, I have noticed that the auras of cats and dogs who are reared in the confines of high rise flats are less harmonious with nature and therefore aurically weakened and of less benefit to their keeper's aura. It's the fine line between domestication and primal instinct that produces the ability for an animal to support its human keeper.

I, no doubt like many other children, sat with my cat on my knee wiping tears away with its tail. Unhygienic, I'm sure, but emotionally gratifying and aurically beneficial. I could see how my cat nurtured me and saw her as my one true friend, someone who loved and understood me.

One afternoon, my father called in to visit while on route to deliver a three-year-old female dog to my brother's young family in a neighbouring town. My nieces had wanted a dog for some time and my father had answered an advertisement in a newspaper on their behalf. The dog seemed to recognise and peer right through me. Within three minutes of this soulful engagement, I realised that she was to live with me. I told my father this and he just laughed and then drove off with the dog. I rushed to the telephone and called my sister-in-law and suggested that if the dog did not fit into her family that she be allowed to come to me.

From the moment the dog arrived at my brother's home she barked and barked and barked, literally driving a wedge between the family and herself. Three weeks later 'Jute', the quick-witted Border collie, came to live with me and we established a friendship that has lasted ten years to date. Even after all this time, she still continues to make loving, thankful gestures towards my brother's family when they visit. Her aura shows that she respects them for letting her go and delivering her to me. Nowadays, instead of rounding up our sheep and goats, she enjoys her retirement by basking in a sunny patch of a paddock, while they graze about her.

The auras of other animals that are easily domesticated can also enhance the human aura through acceptance, affection, and respect.

Recognising sickness in animal auras

You can use your ability to see and understand auras to

recognise the cause of sickness in your pets. This will enable you to seek veterinary advice or to relieve the problem yourself. The following account tells of my cat Barney's survival of a potentially fatal poisoning.

I horrify relatives and friends because I allow snakes to come and sun themselves on the warm bricks of the verandah. On returning home for lunch one day, I saw my pet cat Barney lying stiff and unable to move. At first, I thought he was suffering from sunstroke and so drenched his body with water to lower its temperature. However, the patterns in his aura indicated that something was wrong with his blood. So, I called the vet and described as many symptoms as I could. He promptly diagnosed snakebite and told me that Barney would inevitably die. I thanked him for his professional advice and then attuned myself to Barney's aura to see what he thought of the situation. I found a strong heart and a strong will fighting for survival, so I joined the good fight. I said to myself, 'You're a healer, so heal him.'

My husband mixed up a concoction of Australian Bush Flower essences while I knelt over Barney, channelling all the healing energy I could muster. The hours passed into night and Barney lay in my arms, his gaze fixed and mouth frozen stiff. Tilting his head back we administered the bush essences every hour while I maintained the healing. Out of the blue inspiration came. I went to an old twenty-metre ironbark tree on my property and asked for assistance. I needed all the primal energy charge that I could absorb into my aura. I sat quietly and embraced the tree's gracious energy. With this in store, I sat with Barney in my arms and meditated, then returned him to his sleeping place beside my bed.

In the morning, he made several very small, independent movements. His eyes were sparkling and his mouth was a little more flexible. At regular intervals he was fed glucose and water to boost his physical energy. The following day he was moving his body freely but walked like a drunk. Noticing some stress in his pelvic region I visited the vet who was surprised to find that Barney had survived. The vet diagnosed a full and tense bladder, and showed me how to express it. In the days that followed Barney grew stronger and stronger, regaining his good health. The whole experience has made him more attentive and more devoted to the family. We know, and he knows, that our love saved his life.

Everyone owes it to their aura to let nature clear the cobwebs away. My family chose to exchange the day-to-day inconvenience of living far away from urban resources for the peace and tranquillity of nature. It may take us longer to travel to work and school, but what we come home to makes it well worth it.

Before breakfast each morning, I stand on my back verandah and bid the day good morning. In less than a minute, my dog and cats are at my feet, the ducks quack in reply, the rooster echoes my bidding, the hens cackle, the geese hiss and my rabbit darts around her cage, eagerly awaiting her morning feast of dandelions and snow thistle. This ritual never ceases to entertain and delight me and it keeps my aura healthy.

7

STRENGTHENING AND PROTECTING THE HUMAN AURA

The soul of sweet delight can never be defil'd.

William Blake

The ever-increasing demands of society on the human aura have brought about the decline of its strength, power, health and instinctiveness. Sooner or later we come to realise that as individuals we are more than just flesh and blood. We are vibrant beings, existing in an ever-expanding cosmos. It is then that we go in search of ourselves and reach out to a book such as this.

At no other time in recorded history has the human aura had to cope with such an array of extraneous forces. Human beings once knew how to live with nature intuitively. They understood the weather patterns and animal behaviour, as well as what food to gather for sustenance and healing. They knew that the sun could enhance their energy, but that too much would absorb their life-force. That thundering storms could shatter their energy balance and cause them to feel disjointed. That a fierce howling wind could scatter their energies far and wide leaving them in disarray. They knew what trees could attune their auric body to inspiration and inner wisdom.

No longer do we rely on our instinct and intuition as we once did, and we have distanced ourselves from the etheric (spirit) being that we truly are. Instead, we expect others to take the responsibility for governing our lives. One popular tradition specific to western cultures is the evening news, where consumers anxiously await the advice of the weather report so that the advancing days may be planned. One wonders how much is lost and how much is actually gained as we hurry towards the future.

Foreign auric intrusions are now a daily occurrence due to the numerous electronic devices we have at home and in the workplace. An aura is easily affected by all external vibrational influences as it gives and takes from all energy vibrations in close proximity. It doesn't take much to interfere with its finely woven fabric of electromagnetic particles. Computers, television sets, photocopying machines, microwave ovens and the like, all rearrange the electromagnetic particles of the physical auric layer. If a person is exposed to these appliances for a long period of time, which most people in western society are, they can be left feeling washed out and run down.

Mobile telephones have a fascinating, but destructive, effect on the aura. Not only do they rearrange the electromagnetic particles of the aura, but in addition they create circular wave-like motions that pulsate rapidly around the ears and head. Constant users could find themselves suffering physically from ear pressure, headaches or eye defects. Knowing this, everyone in my family holds their mobile phone on the outer edge of their etheric body, and are sure to limit their use.

I find it particularly fascinating the way most of the general population chooses to relax. Thousands of people head off to the beach and other holiday sites, season after season, unaware of how they can and can't really relax. Caravan parks and island resorts are crammed full of people all seeking the same goal: to free themselves of the stresses of everyday life—

to get away from it all. While it is true that they are free of their usual social aura and so feel relaxed, their auras are still busily interacting with many others, thus not allowing true revitalisation. Consequently, when the holidaymakers return home to the workforce, their prior state of fatigue quickly returns.

It's wise to remember that we are all vulnerable to the ever-changing energy patterns of the aura as it lives and breathes, soaking up the world around us, so we must find suitable ways to maintain the self and bring it to peace.

Our ancestors coped only with the impingement of relationships, climatic changes and the trials of survival. Today, we have all that (in a different way) plus more to contend with. Therefore, I cannot stress enough the emphasis that we all need to place on strengthening and protecting the aura for our total well-being.

Take an objective look at your lifestyle as it, too, can have a major impact on the well-being of your aura. Traumatic relationships at home or at work can throw the aura into disarray, creating an inability to focus and overcome the situation. Poor self-esteem can create a vulnerability which allows stronger personality types to dominate you. Medication, such as painkillers, antibiotics and psychiatric drugs distort the aura. All work and no play stifles the aura, causing it to shrink and decay, as does depression. A poor diet, when reflected in the physical layer of the aura, prevents the vital layer of the aura from rejuvenating itself. Consequently emotional and physical ill health prevails.

Strengthening your aura

At times you may say to yourself, 'I'm not feeling myself today.' This is because your body is intuitively telling you that its energy is out of balance and in need of rejuvenation. If you hear yourself say, 'I need some personal space', the body is intuitively informing you of auric shrinkage. On the contrary, when you think, 'I feel like myself today', it's because your energy has been recharged and brought back into balance. The exercises in this section will help you to keep your aura strong and balanced.

The following self-destructive agents need to be addressed in order for you to strengthen your aura:

- Poor self-esteem
- Belittling the self
- Disruptive relationships
- Constant negativity/depression
- Addictive poor diet (sugar/chocolate/tea/coffee/cigarettes)
- Lack of regular exercise
- Tiredness and lack of rest
- Lack of contact with nature and fresh air
- Alcohol/drugs/psychiatric medication
- Lack of commitment to self-development.

Determining the strength of your aura

Before you can work on strengthening your aura you need to determine its current strength or vulnerability. The following exercise will give you an indication of the state of your aura.

Exercise

Place the number [1] in the boxes which apply to you, then total your score.

[   ]   A particular person at home or work drains you or makes you feel a failure.

[   ]   The screams of children at play annoy you.

[ ] Some people literally give you the shivers.

[ ] Repetitive noises, like tapping and grinding, irritate you.

[ ] When criticised, you go within your shell.

[ ] You don't speak up for yourself.

[ ] You don't like to be made a fuss of or touched.

[ ] You continually argue with yourself when trying to make a decision.

[ ] Nobody seems to listen to you or understand you.

[ ] You always seem to be singled out or blamed.

[ ] Relationships never seem to work out the way you expected them to.

[ ] Everything you want to do seems to escape you.

[ ] When you feel low, it takes hours, or even days, to overcome the depression.

[ ] You are concerned about what people think of you.

[ ] Your expectations of other people are rarely fulfilled.

[ ] Dreams are greatly impressed on your mind and emotions for days.

[ ] You are searching for the key to happiness.

[ ] Sitting in front of the television or a computer for an hour or more tires you.

[ ] Large crowds make you feel congested or closed in.

[ ] A day in the city makes you feel tired and worn out.

[ ] You visit a friend when tired and confused and within moments feel much better.

[ ] Theatre and festival outings make you feel tired.

[ ] An overcast or rainy day depresses you.

[ ] Your batteries are recharged walking along an isolated beach or through a forest.

[ ] Water renews your sense of well-being.

[ ] You are enhanced by those with whom you share your home.

[ ] Everyone seems to like you and you make friends easily.

[ ] You laugh and sing a lot.

[ ] You make people smile.

How did you score?

(15–29)   The aura is open and vulnerable.
(8–14)   The aura is overcoming weakness.
(1–7)   The aura has a balanced strength.

Do you have a lot of work to do on yourself in order to strengthen your aura and awaken your intuitive skills? If so go over the questionnaire again and also compile your own list of intolerances and weaknesses. The other exercises within this book are designed to help you out. Did you discover that you are easily drained? If so, you are opened aurically and your emotions are very vulnerable. This can only be fixed by overcoming major personal fears.

Wounding the aura

The fiercest enemy of your body, spirit and aura is the emotional and destructive mind. Learning to strengthen and protect your aura through the balance of thought is a vital recipe for personal happiness. The way in which you express yourself reinforces your beliefs and creates your reality. This is because your body believes every word you say. If your mind suggests that you pick up a ball, you do so. If your mind suggests that you hold a cup with both hands so that it won't drop, you do just that. This occurs with every other thought and feeling the mind receives.

Negative words and self-expressions deplete the aura due to the emotional energy it absorbs. Correct negative patterns by replacing frequently used words with their opposites. Life is an adventure *not* life is a drag.

Exercise

Take a look at the following words to determine how often you wound yourself daily:

- too good for me
- I'm sick of trying

- what if?
- stupid idiot
- thick-skinned
- no way, I couldn't do that
- thin-skinned
- what have I got to offer?
- I swallow my feelings
- I'm a hopeless case
- bite your tongue
- I can't
- swallow your pride
- I wish I were dead

- a glutton for punishment
- nobody likes me
- an accident waiting to happen
- I'm ugly
- a walking time bomb
- I hate myself
- eat your heart out
- I'm boring
- it's not fair
- who'd give me a go?
- I will never amount to anything
- brainless.

Listen to what you are saying during a conversation with others to monitor your self-talk, which clearly defines your level of self-esteem, self-destructiveness and what personal weakness you keep re-inforcing. It's amazing just how much negativity creeps into general conversation. Be a super sleuth and flush out your weak points.

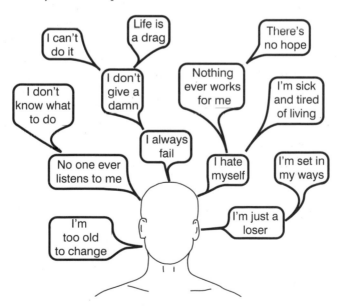

Affirming the aura

Make a pact to listen to yourself and to correct your negative thoughts and words. Introduce an appropriate auric affirmation into your life. By harnessing the power of the mind, you can alter its perspective and create the most wonderful reality.

Select one or more of the following affirmations and exclaim them out loud to yourself. Repeat the affirmation with sincerity and confidence several times throughout the day, for a period of fifteen to thirty days. Over this time the message will have lodged firmly in your mind. Then allow time to reveal to you what changes the power of your mind can create.

MY AURA IS BALANCED AND WHOLE
Encourages the mind to activate its self-alignment power and thus achieve its goal.

MY AURA GIVES AND RECIVES IN A BALANCED WAY
Helps you to prevent yourself being aurically drained, and you draining others.

MY AURA COMMUNICATES WITH OTHERS
Nurtures those in need of friendship and attracts new friends.

MY AURA GENERATES NEW LIFE
Aids in the correction of ill health, emotional disorders and poor realities.

MY AURA IS A HEALING TOOL FOR OTHERS
Aids in the healing of loved ones.

MY AURA IS AN EVOLVING ENERGY
Encourages self-development of the mind, body and spirit.

MY AURA IS WOVEN INTO THE FABRIC OF LIFE
Facilitates unity with the world around you.

How to permanently strengthen your aura

As you can see, some very necessary changes to your life and health may be warranted. A balanced lifestyle is what every aura seeks. It brims over with fulfilment when exchanging with nature and loved ones. It is stimulated when in the company of inspiring, charismatic individuals. Below I have highlighted nine easy steps by which you can permanently strengthen your aura.

1. Practise random acts of kindness.
2. Be affectionate.
3. Smile and laugh a lot.
4. Develop your creativity.
5. Like yourself for your individuality.
6. Intake fresh air daily.
7. Eat a balanced organic diet.
8. Meditate daily.
9. Make peace with yourself.

Auric strengthening techniques for immediate results

Here are four exercises which offer immediate auric revitalisation in times of stress when you are overwhelmed with responsibility, drained by negative people or situations and poor health. Exercises one and two if practised weekly and over a period of six months or more will have long-term beneficial effects.

Exercises

EXERCISE ONE

Find a quiet place indoors where you will not be disturbed and plan to spend a minimum of one hour there in isolation. To avoid any auric interaction be certain that there are no animals, plants, people or electric gadgets nearby. You can relax and read a good book or simply daydream. The isolation from extraneous energy forces allows the aura to realign itself, giving you the sensation of being 'all together' once again. Longer stints of isolation strengthen and align the aura even more.

EXERCISE TWO

1. Sit comfortably under the canopy of a mature tree.
2. Close your eyes and take several deep breaths to relax the body.
3. Feel the energy of the tree filling your lungs with new life, with every breath you take.
4. Feel the aura expand outwards, upwards and downwards. Allow your senses to feel the life-force of the tree. Become one with the tree.

EXERCISE THREE

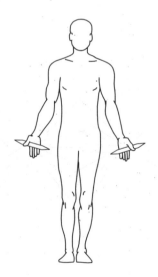

AURA ENHANCEMENT WITH CRYSTALS

Two double-terminated quartz crystals (white or pink) can be used to temporarily boost your auric energy levels.

1. Stand upright, or sit, with your feet slightly apart.
2. Hold a double-terminated quartz crystal in each hand.
3. Breathe deeply and slowly to release any built-up pockets of tension.
4. Focus your mind on your hand chakras to activate the crystals' energy. Feel the auric energy in your hand chakras penetrate and combine with the energy of the crystals. As the two connect, the crystals will radiate their energy, expanding into the complete auric body. When your palms begin to tingle, enhancement has begun. You will have a sense of electric-like currents running through your mind, body and spirit. The crystals will temporarily supplement your normal energy levels.
5. Absorb this energy into your aura for ten minutes.

EXERCISE FOUR

1. Lie on the floor with pillows under your head, knees and the arch of your back.
2. Close your eyes and take three slow, gentle deep breaths to release body tension.
3. Lie perfectly still and quiet and focus on your breath. Feel the energy radiating from your chakras.
4. Direct the energy to completely fill and expand the physical and etheric layers of the aura.
5. Feel the energy rising upwards, filtering through the remaining layers of the aura.

The weekly aura workout for rejuvenation

This is how I maintain my aura and how I encourage my friends to do so. We all know that the key to good health is a balanced diet, exercise and living free of stress. A new dimension in this prescription is to keep your aura replenished by spending one hour by yourself each day. My motto is an hour each day keeps ill health at bay.

This simple routine helps to ensure clarity of mind, focus, well-being, stamina and inner peace.

- Spend two hours, a half or a full day by yourself to recharge your auric resources.
- Be sure to surround yourself with colours that emotionally lift you.
- Immerse yourself in inspirational music to resonate and affirm positivity through your physical and less emotional body.
- Sit under the canopy of a mature tree for an hour or so and breathe in its natural balance.
- Select six kind words and plan to use them frequently in conversations with friends and family.
- Be certain to keep company with inspirational and stimulating people.
- Be prepared to let life work for you. Don't be a slave to it!

Protecting the aura

Frequently people ask me to show them how to protect their aura against negative people and situations. Protecting the aura other than by way of developing good self-esteem is difficult. There are temporary measures that can help you in a vulnerable situation, but ultimately they change the patterns of the aura if continually used. One such method is known as masking.

Masking and sealing the aura

When you mask your aura you are inhibiting another person's ability to interpret your aura correctly, by giving off a signal that you are difficult to reach and penetrate. It is a very useful technique in some circumstances, but be warned, if used continually it will eventually mask the aura so much that no one (friend or foe) will feel that they can communicate with you. You will hear people say, 'I don't know what it is, but I just can't seem to get through to you any more.' This can have a devastating effect on relationships and you will have to work very hard to reverse the situation.

METHOD ONE

1. Sit upright with your feet crossed at the ankles.
2. Clasp your hands together and cross your thumbs.
3. Place in the groin area.

This method instantly masks the physical and spiritual layers of the aura and prevents you from being drained. The block will last for as long as you maintain the position. I have noticed that many people sit this way on public transport or in a meeting. Many of them don't consciously realise what they are doing, but it works all the same.

METHOD TWO

1. Sit upright in a comfortable chair.
2. Close your eyes and take three very deep breaths.
3. Feel your body relax with each breath.
4. Picture a swirling white light hovering above your head.
5. Feel it gently swirl its way slowly down your body, forming a spiral mask of your aura.

This mask will cause the people in your life to stand back from you. The same exercise using gold light will help protect the aura from being drained by preying spirits.

METHOD THREE

1. Sit upright in a comfortable chair. Close your eyes and take five deep breaths and feel your body relax more and more with every breath.
2. Picture a purple and pearl light cascading from the third eye and crown chakras and flowing slowly down your body.

3. Feel it twist and turn to secure the mask underneath your feet.

This mask will give off a vibration of distance from reality.

SEALING THE AURA

To create a mask which seals and shields the aura, visualise a coloured energy in your mind in the shape of a triangle, bubble or cylinder and imagine that it is surrounding your body.

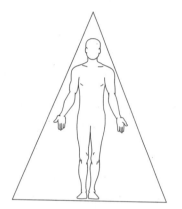

Triangular seal

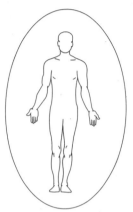

Bubble seal

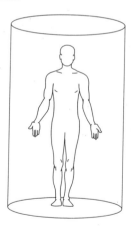

Cylindrical seal

Refreshing the aura

If you answer yes to one or more of the following questions, your aura definitely needs refreshing. Regular self-cleansing of the aura to rid it of energy debris caused by interaction with friends and family, or other energy vibrations, is essential to your well-being. Sexual intercourse, in particular, can carry with it intense debris due to its intimacy.

- Do you ever feel that you wear other people's worries, frustrations or fears?
- Do you carry the weight of the world on your shoulders?
- Are you stuck in a rut?
- Do other people get you down?
- Do you travel by public transport?
- Do you have a mobile telephone to keep you in touch with your work?
- Can you work a computer?
- Do you spend a lot of time watching television or playing video games?
- Is the majority of your daily intake of food microwaved?

The technological age is an asset if you know how to use it. While writing this book on my speedy computer, I left my study every two hours to play on my garden swing. Swaying back and forth high above the ground in the freshness of the country air, my aura opened to the wholeness of nature which cleansed and restored it, facilitating creative focus.

A few weeks prior to Christmas 1995, I asked Santa Claus (my bearded husband) for a park-size swing for me to use to clear away the auric cobwebs. He had his father install it while we were working away from home, to surprise me on Christmas Day. On Christmas morning I was led down the long and winding garden path to find it nestled between a huge mulberry tree and a Granny Smith apple tree, so I would not go hungry while soaring through the air for long periods at a time! Its hand-painted fiery red seat, to inspire creativity, caught my immediate attention as it captured the rays of the early morning sun. The swing was positioned so that if I sat facing north I could talk to the sheep and goats grazing in the paddock, or if I sat facing the south I could look over the swimming pool as well as rear and side courtyards of the house. Either way I am in communion with life.

My personal research on the effectiveness of swings has proven a wonderful healing tool for city people. If you visit a nearby park in the early hours of the morning or the late hours of the evening, you will generally find a degree of tranquillity and isolation. A twenty minute auric workout on a swing will tone the muscles in your legs, thighs, chest, arms and shoulders. It will expand the lungs, and, last but not least, cleanse and refresh your aura. Much more enjoyable than pumping iron!

The 'get fit' movement tends to overlook the etheric body in the search for holistic health. Therefore, many people achieve physical health, but remain imbalanced in their emotions, mind and spirit.

Self-cleansing vortex technique

The exercise that follows is a simple method of refreshing your aura at any time of the day. It is an ideal daily routine for healers.

Exercise

1. Sit or stand comfortably.
2. Breathe slowly and deeply until you have relaxed every muscle in your body.
3. Imagine, in your mind's eye, a spinning web of clear, sparkling diamond light energy gently swirling its way towards you.

4. Allow it to extend fifteen metres or more around your body. Spinning clockwise, it will draw closer, firmly embracing around the body. The strongest force of the energy is at the top of your head. As the energy moves its way slowly spinning through the body (at each chakra point), extraneous energies are being removed.

5. Allow the energy to exit through the soles of your feet.

At every alternative health festival there is at least one healer advocating aura cleansing and balancing. I see people brush a person's aura as if it were a knotted head of hair. I've watched as their hands move over the aura in swirling motions as if it were a conglomeration of ingredients waiting to be mixed and then set. I see them dip their hands into the etheric layer of the aura, as if it were a child's lucky dip, reaching deep to find the prize. I hear them tell wild and woolly tales of their adventures into the mysterious world of the human aura.

You can make a difference

In your attempt to strengthen and protect your own aura, don't forget that your aura affects others too, which can be measured by their behaviour towards you. Being aurically responsible in the fast pace of modern society is a step in the right direction. Responsibility begins with each individual. If everyone in the world was receptive to this idea, perhaps we would see greater harmony in the way we communicate.

Frequently people describe to me a relationship with a friend, relative or workmate which is draining them to the point of frustration and fatigue. I immediately respond by asking them to reflect on the weaknesses in their own aura which allows so much energy to be zapped from them. You should ask yourself why your aura can't withstand the challenge? We are quick to blame others for 'rubbing us up the wrong way' when in fact we may be the cause. As William

Blake, the poet and philosopher, so aptly put it, 'The fox condemns the trap, not himself.'

It pays to remember at all times that your aura is a walking, talking advertisement of who you are and therefore consciously attracts what you need to learn in order to expand your life experience. Painful encounters are an excellent example. Although life may take you to what seems like hell and back, you grow from this learning, often witnessing many dramatic changes in your life. In the general web of life, the imbalances we feel from time to time are due to the interaction of our aura with other auras, which are either only partially able, or completely unable, to fulfil our demands for balance.

You can change a disruptive environment by keeping your aura in balance and attuned to unity through consciously vibrating good emanations. Thinking positive thoughts, affirming corrective change and wishing the offending person well, sets up a protective screen in your aura while at the same time this offers a healing exchange to the offender. At all times avoid becoming embroiled in an exchange of negative words or emotions. Should a situation occur that is difficult to avoid, keep a metre between yourself and the offender to ensure that the brunt of disruptive energy being directed towards you is inhibited, thus limiting the penetration of emotional shock waves through your aura. This defence technique also helps the aura to recover rapidly.

I advised a mother who was complaining of continual difficulty with her teenage daughter to gather the family to sit together in a circle, holding hands and focusing their thoughts on empowering the girl's reality. Her nerves had become frayed due to the anticipation of sitting her final school examinations. The family performed this exercise together every night for a week prior to the exams, and it instilled self-confidence in the girl, through the love and support exhibited by her family. The mother also felt that family unity had greatly increased. Aura blending with focused attention always produces positive results, sometimes instantly.

Centre your energies daily through meditation or by using the self-cleansing vortex technique (see page 184). Then you can rest assured that you will be radiating healthy, balanced and well-meaning auric vibrations that can confidently give and take without depleting your own energies.

As you advance, so does your aura.
As you retreat, so does it.
It is a living force.
The true reflection of who you really are.

8

TWENTY COMMON QUESTIONS

Whenever I teach my aura course, the participants always ask me numerous questions about auras. As a quick reference, I have compiled twenty of the most commonly asked questions along with a brief answer. Some of these questions are discussed in more detail in the text.

WHAT IS AN AURA?

The human aura is comprised of seven layers of electromagnetic particles suspended around the body. The first three layers contour the body's shape, whereas the outer four layers form a colourful egg shape.

WHEN DOES THE AURA FIRST FORM?

At conception the union of the egg and sperm produces a unique energy pattern which sparks the development of the personal aura. As the foetus grows its aura reflects its total being.

WHAT HAPPENS TO THE AURA WHEN YOU DIE?

The aura fades to nothing at the point of death. Only the etheric layer remains and lives on, forming a ghost of yourself.

CAN EVERYONE SEE AURAS?

Auric vision is a natural part of the human psyche. Most people unknowingly use it daily at a subconscious level to make assessments about people and life in general.

HOW DO YOU SEE AN AURA?

The human eye when combined with the inner eye, i.e. the intuitive self, can easily view an aura. The rods and cones of the human eye detect auric colour and light vibrations, while the inner eye intuitively interprets their meanings. Therefore, both sight and intuition must be in harmony to see an aura.

DO YOU SEE AURAS IN FOCUS OR A HAZE?

At a distance of two to three metres an aura appears as a mass of transparent colour. However, on close examination it consists of tiny pinhead dots of colours magnetically suspended together, which can be interpreted.

CAN YOU FEEL AN AURA?

The electromagnetic particles of the aura's physical layer (the layer closest to the body) can easily be felt when the palms of the hands are rubbed together vigorously, then slowly and gently separated to experience the magnetic tug.

IS THE AURA PATTERNED?

Odd shapes, stripes, wiggly lines and blotches appear in the aura regularly. They indicate everything from illness to pregnancy.

WHAT DO THE COLOUR VARIATIONS OF THE AURA MEAN?

Colour in the aura forms as a direct result of personal and environmental experiences, and represents encounters of the mind, body and spirit.

DOES COLOURED OR PATTERNED CLOTHING AFFECT THE AURA?

Colours in the environment vibrate into the aura and

produce a warming or cooling affect. For example, when you wear the colour red it will cause every trace of red in the aura to vibrate at a higher frequency. Most people instinctively wear clothing that resembles the dominant colour patterns in their aura. Black and grey are the only shades that can have a negative affect. They have a tendency to restrict peak performance by absorbing the light and energy of the aura.

WHAT CAN AN AURA TELL YOU ABOUT YOURSELF?

The aura is a reflection of everything you think, feel and experience in the past, present and future, therefore the aura is an advertisement of yourself. Clairvoyants are quickly able to glean information about you and make predictions by interpreting your auric vibrations.

HOW OFTEN DOES AN AURA CHANGE?

An aura changes as slowly or rapidly as you, yourself. Colours which relate to the emotions change quickly, while colours which represent personal strength, achievement and destiny alter slowly.

HOW DO WE AFFECT EACH OTHER'S AURAS?

Auric energy interacts with all forms of energy. When two people meet their auras exchange energy, indicating instinctively whether there is like or dislike. Some people drain you of energy because their aura exchanges their imbalance with your balance.

DO INANIMATE OBJECTS HAVE AURAS?

No. However, if a person has been handling an object, a resonance of the human aura remains for up to seventy-two hours, giving off an impression that the object has an aura.

HOW CAN SOMEONE LEARN TO SEE AN AURA?

Firstly, you must attune to and exercise the creative side of your brain. Secondly, you must expand your intuitive senses. And thirdly, you must allow the aura to materialise in front of you and not search for it with the hard stare of the eyes.

HOW IS NATURAL AURIC VISION DISCOURAGED OR STIFLED?

Where there is a lack of creative stimulation a person will have difficulty connecting with their auric vision.

DOES AGE INHIBIT A PERSON'S ABILITY TO SEE AURAS?

Only subdued creative and intuitive expression inhibit auric vision. A person can regain their auric vision at any age.

HOW DO YOU STRENGTHEN AN AURA?

Self-esteem is the foundation for long term auric strength and balance. Self-respect and self-confidence produce strong, vibrant colours.

WHEN HAVING AN AURA READING WHAT COLOUR CLOTHING SHOULD YOU WEAR?

White clothing is non-invasive and allows a clear view of the colours of the aura as they drape the body.

HOW CAN I TELL IF AN AURA READING IS TRUE AND CORRECT?

Part of the reading will relate to your present life events and it is therefore easy to personally assess the reading's accuracy. However, the remainder of the reading will relate to the future and can only be confirmed then.

RESOURCES

EARTHKEEPERS HEALING SANCTUARY

The Earthkeepers Healing Sanctuary in Australia coordinates Judith Collins' private consultations and courses nationally and internationally as well as offering spiritual healing, books and CDs.

45 Addison Street
Thirlmere
New South Wales
2572
Australia

Tel: (0061) 02 4681 9623
Fax: (0061) 02 4681 8280
http://www.earthkeepers.com.au